A SERIES GUIDE TO CONNOISSEURSHIP & TASTE

Through the lens of the connoisseur,

We collate, curate and narrate the journey of art across the cultures, genres and history,

Inspiring a new generation of thinkers who will in turn be woven into the tapestry of art.

鑑賞家 CONNOISSEUR
DISCOVER ART OF APPRECIATION

Copyright© 2024. James B. S. All Rights Reserved.

No part of this work covered by the copyright herein may be reproduced or used in any form or by any means—graphic, electronic, or mechanical without the prior written permission of the publisher. any request for photocopying, recording, taping, or information storage and retrieval systems of any part of this book shall be directed in writing to the author.

This publication contains the opinions and ideas of its author(s) and is designed to provide useful advice in regard to the subject matter covered.

CASE ID: 1-14294904651
ISBN: 978-1-965407-55-4

Editor-in-Chief: James B. S.

Senior Editor: Scott Brooks

Art Consultant: Salina H.Y. Shih

Marketing & PR: Vanessa Qu

WWW.CONNOISSEUR.CC

Cover photograph by James B. S.

Contents

Three Mona Lisa 1

Renaissance Man and His Collection 13

East meets West 49

The Recital of the Future 69

Smile 75

Art Tour of Puerto Vallarta 145

three Mona Lisa

-By James B.S.

The Mona Lisa, housed in the Louvre Museum in Paris, is undoubtedly one of the most famous and recognizable paintings in the world. Created by Leonardo da Vinci between 1503 and 1519, it has fascinated conoscenti and general audiences for centuries.

The subject is Lisa Gherardini, who was the wife of a wealthy Florentine merchant named Francesco del Giocondo. Hence the Italian name of the painting is 'La Gioconda,' 'the joyful one.' But the discovery of Gherardini's identity is only recent, and was successful thanks to three key pieces of evidence.

Portrait of Lisa Gherardini, wife of Francesco del Giocondo, known as the Mona Lisa or Monna Lisa, oil on wood (poplar), 1503-1519 CE, Dimension in centimeters: 79.4 (H) x 53.4 (W)
LEONARDO DA VINICI (Leonardo di ser Piero da Vinci, known as Leonardo da Vinci) (1452 -1519 CE)
Paris, Musée du Louvre, Inventory number: INV 779/MR 316

The earliest source is a book published in 1550, 'Lives of the most excellent painters, sculptors and architects', by Giorgio Vasari (1511-1574).

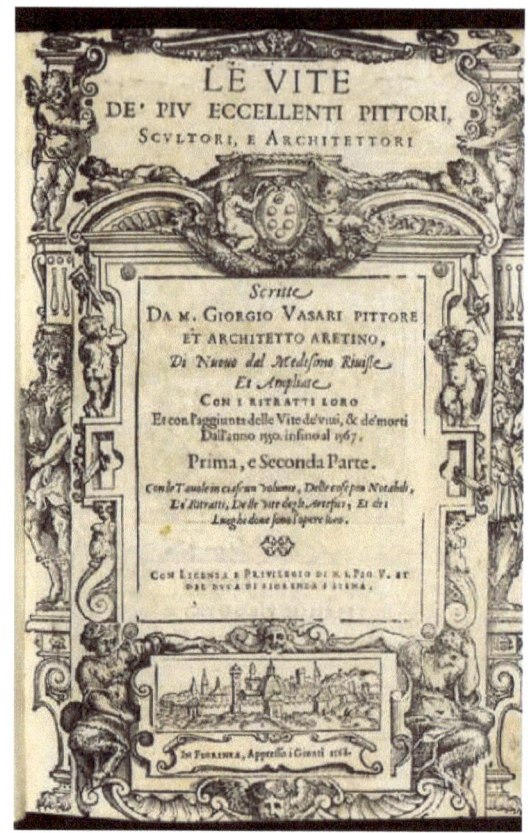

Cover of 'The Lives of the Most Excellent Painters, Sculptors, and Architects', 1568 edition

Vasari is considered to be the first art historian, and he was highly prolific, working as a painter, architect and, effectively, the minister of culture to the Medici court in Florence.

Of Leonardo's painting he writes, 'Leonardo undertook for Francesco del Giocondo to make the portrait of his wife Mona Lisa and left it unfinished after having labored for four years, which work is today with the King of France in Fontainebleau.'

Portrait of Giorgio Vasari, Attributed to Jacopo Zucchi (1542-1596), Oil on wood, dimension in centimeters: 100.5 (H) x 80 (W), Florence, Uffizi Gallery, accession number: 00021975

A margin note, discovered in the University Library of Heidelberg, which proved that Lisa del Giocondo was the subject of Mona Lisa

Our second source comes from records in the Florentine archives. These were discovered by scholar Giuseppe Pallanti, and indicate that Francesco del Giocondo commissioned a portrait of his wife, Lisa, around the same time Leonardo was known to be painting the 'Mona Lisa.'

The third and final piece of evidence was discovered in 2005 at the Heidelberg Library, on a margin note handwritten by Agostino Vespucci in his copy of Cicero's Epistulae ad Familiares. In it, he compares Leonardo to Apelles, a famous painter of Ancient Greece: 'Apelles the painter. That is the way Leonardo da Vinci does it with all of his pictures, like, for example, with the countenance of Lisa del Giocondo and that of Anne, the mother of the Virgin. We will see how he is going to do it regarding the great council chamber, the thing which he has just come to terms with the Gonfaloniere. October 1503.'

The provenance of the painting has excited less discussion than the subject's smile, however, which has been the subject of countless interpretations and studies. Observers note that it appears to change when viewed from different angles, and that the eyes, too, seem to follow the viewer's movements.

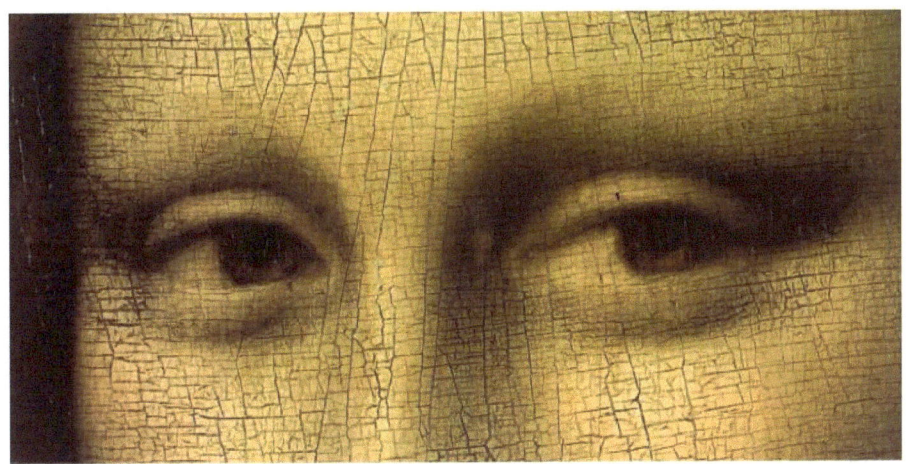

The depiction of the mouth and eyes demonstrates Leonardo's mastery of sfumato, a technique invented by him to blend colors and tones for creating a soft, blurred effect. The term sfumato ('blurred' or 'faded') comes from the Italian sfumare, meaning to tone down or evaporate like smoke.

Sfumato allowed Leonardo to explore the interplay of light and shadow (chiaroscuro) with remarkable subtlety, enhancing the naturalism of his paintings.

The effect is achieved by applying multiple thin layers of translucent glaze, allowing for seamless transitions between light and shadow. This method avoids harsh lines and borders, giving the subject a lifelike and three-dimensional appearance.

Numerous artists during and after the Renaissance adopted sfumato. It became a fundamental technique in Western art, inspiring painters like Raphael, Correggio, and later Baroque artists who further developed chiaroscuro and tenebrism.

Sfumato revolutionized portrait-painting and helped create a more realistic and emotionally engaging representation of subjects. It allowed artists to depict the human face with greater softness and complexity.

To be continued...
(In the next volume we will continue explore the Mona Lisa in Louvre and other two Mona Lisa)

Image Source:
Leonardo da Vinci, Portrait of Lisa Gherardini, wife of Francesco del Giocondo, known as the Mona Lisa or Monna Lisa, oil on wood (poplar), 1503-1519. Dimensions in centimeters: 79.4 (H) x 53.4 (W), Paris, Musée du Louvre, Inventory number:INV 779/MR 316, collections.louvre.fr/en/ark:/53355/cl010062370#

Cover of 'The Lives of the Most Excellent Painters, Sculptors, and Architects', 1568 edition, commons.wikimedia.org/wiki/File:Vite.jpg

Jacopo Zucchi (1542-1596) (attrib.), Portrait of Giorgio Vasari, Oil on wood, dimensions in centimeters: 100.5 (H) x 80 (W), Florence, Uffizi Gallery, accession number: 00021975, commons.wikimedia.org/wiki/File:Zucchi,_Jacopo_-_Vasari,_Giorgio_-_Uffizi_ICCD.jpg

A margin note, discovered in the University Library of Heidelberg, which proved that Lisa del Giocondo was the subject of Mona Lisa, Heidelberg University Library, commons.wikimedia.org/wiki/File:Mona_Lisa_margin_scribble.jpg

Francesco Melzi (attrib.), Portrait of Leonardo da Vinci (this portrait is the only certain contemporary depiction of Leonardo), Drawing, Dimensions in centimeters: 27.5 (H) x 19 (W), Royal Collection, United Kingdom, Accession number: RCIN 912726 commons.wikimedia.org/wiki/File:Francesco_Melzi_-_Portrait_of_Leonardo.png

Portrait of Leonardo da Vinci (c.1515-1518), Drawing, Attributed to Francesco Melzi, Dimension in centimeters: 27.5 (H) x 19 (W), Royal Collection, United Kingdom, Accession number: RCIN 912726

This portrait is the only certain contemporary depiction of Leonardo

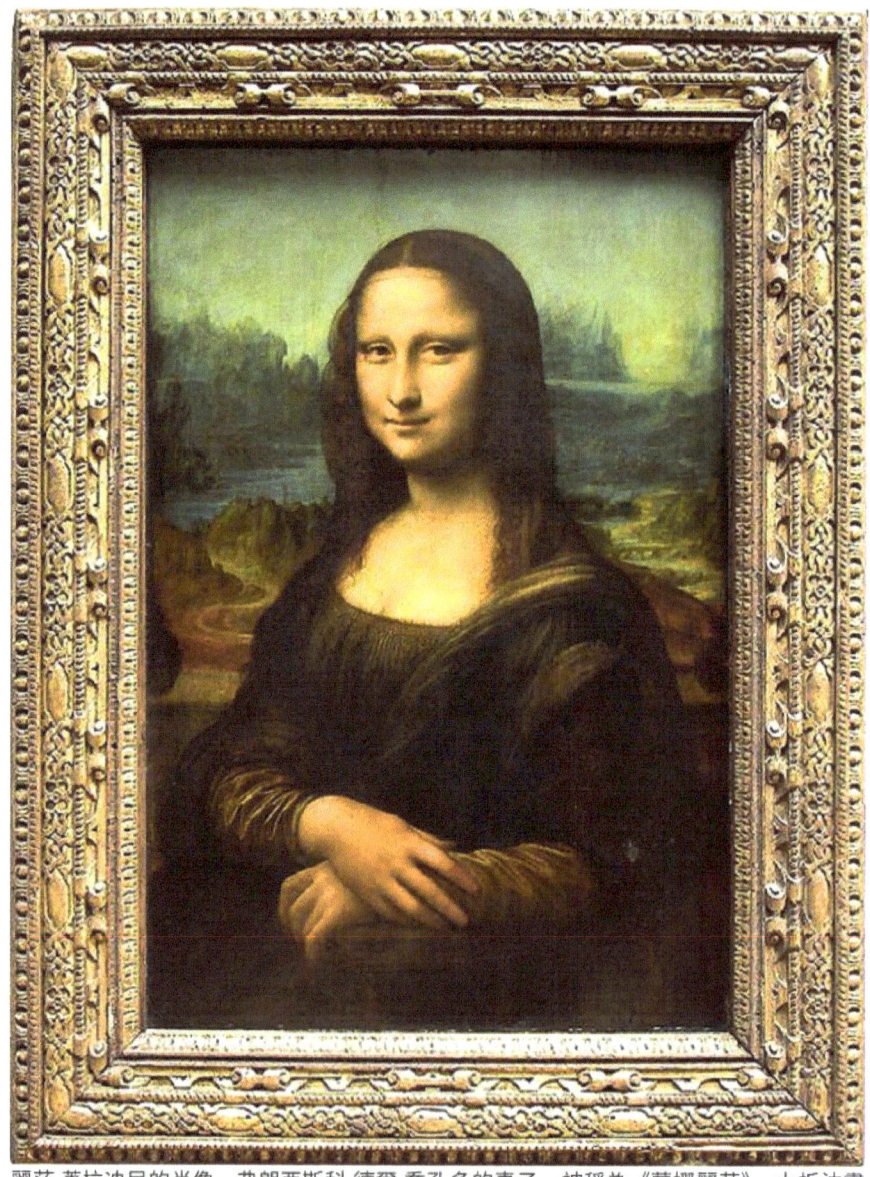

麗莎·蓋拉迪尼的肖像，弗朗西斯科·德爾·喬孔多的妻子，被稱為《蒙娜麗莎》，木板油畫（楊木）1503-1519年，規格(厘米)：79.4（高）x 53.4（寬）
列奧納多·達·芬奇（Leonardo di ser Piero da Vinci）(1452-1519年)，巴黎，卢浮宫，藏品编号：INV 779/MR 316

三幅蒙娜麗莎

收藏於巴黎羅浮宮博物館的《蒙娜麗莎》無疑是世界上最著名和最受認可的畫作之一。這幅傑作由達芬奇於1503年至1519年間創作，幾個世紀以來一直是令人著迷的艺术标志。

畫中的女士是麗莎·蓋拉迪尼 (Lisa Gherardini)，她是佛羅倫薩富商弗朗西斯科·德爾·喬孔多 (Francesco del Giocondo) 的妻子。因此，這幅畫的義大利名字是"La Gioconda"，意思是"快樂的人"。

蒙娜麗莎的人物鑑定基於三個交叉證據。首先根據喬治·瓦薩裡 (Giorgio Vasari) 於1550年出版《最優秀畫家、雕塑家和建築師的傳記》中的紀錄。

喬治·瓦薩裡（Giorgio Vasari，1511-1574年）被認為是"第一位藝術史學家"，他是一位畫家、建築師，實際上是佛羅倫薩美第奇宮廷的文化部長（以現在稱為而言）。他在書中寫道："弗朗西斯科·德爾·喬孔多委託列奧納多，為他的妻子蒙娜麗莎繪製肖像，但在四年後仍未完成，該作品今天被法國國王蒐藏於楓丹白露。"

其次，根據佛羅倫薩檔案館的記錄，包括學者朱塞佩·帕蘭蒂（Giuseppe Pallanti）發現的檔案，表明弗朗西斯科·德爾·喬孔多委託為他的妻子麗莎繪製肖像，與列奧納多開始畫《蒙娜麗莎》在同一時期。

第三個證據是 2005 年在德國海德堡大學圖書館發現的，出現在阿戈斯蒂諾·韋斯普奇 (Agostino Vespucci) 書中的旁注中。他將列奧納多與古希臘著名畫家阿佩萊斯進行了比較："列奧納多·達·芬奇如畫家阿佩萊斯所做，以這樣的方式處理所有的畫作，例如麗莎·德爾·喬孔多和聖母瑪利亞的母親安妮的面容。我們將看看他將如何處理偉大的議會廳，這是他剛剛與總督達成協議的事情。1503 年 10 月"

蒙娜麗莎神秘的微笑一直是無數詮釋和研究的主題。從不同的角度看，它似乎會呈現不同的笑意。蒙娜麗莎的目光，無論觀眾走到哪裡，似乎都會跟隨著他們。整幅作品創造出與眾不同的迷人而親密的體驗。

蒙娜麗莎的嘴巴和眼睛的描繪證明了達芬奇對暈染法的掌握，這是他發明的一種混合顏色和色調以創造柔和、模糊效果的技術。來自義大利語"sfumare"，意思是減弱或像煙霧一樣蒸發。

暈染法讓列奧納多能夠以非凡的微妙方式探索光與影的相互作用（明暗對比），增強了畫作的自然主義風格。

列奧納多透過應用多層薄薄的半透明油彩來實現這種效果，他使光與影之間產生無縫過渡。這種方法避免了粗糙的線條和邊框，賦予主體逼真的三維外觀。

暈染法徹底革新了肖像畫，創造了更真實自然、更富情感表現力的肖像。它使藝術家能夠以更柔和細膩的方式描繪人像。

文藝復興時期和之後的許多藝術家都採用暈染法。它成為西方藝術的基本技巧，啟發了拉斐爾、科雷喬等畫家，以及後來進一步發展明暗對比和暗色主義的巴洛克藝術家。

待續...
下一冊我們將繼續探索羅浮宮的《蒙娜麗莎》以及另外兩幅《蒙娜麗莎》

Phil Nuytten with Bill Holm pole at Nuytten residence,
photograph courtesy of the Nuytten Family

'Renaissance Man' and his collection

-By Jeanette Langmann

Phil Nuytten, was a pioneer in many fields - underwater explorer and subsea engineer, inventor, marine archaeologist, tech manufacturer, businessman, songwriter, carver, author, native advocate, and avid collector.

He is often referred to as a 'Renaissance man', because of his diverse interests and abilities.

The National Geographic Society's publication, 'Exploring the Deep Frontier' described: 'A creative engineer himself, Phil combines an impressive record of commercial diving experience and a disarming sense of humor with the skills of an artist and the talents of a professional magician'.

Dr. Joseph MacInnis, eminent Canadian underwater explorer in his book 'The Breadalbane Story', said 'Phil is one of those extraordinary characters who, because of his wide range of skills and knowledge, seems to have surfaced from another century'.

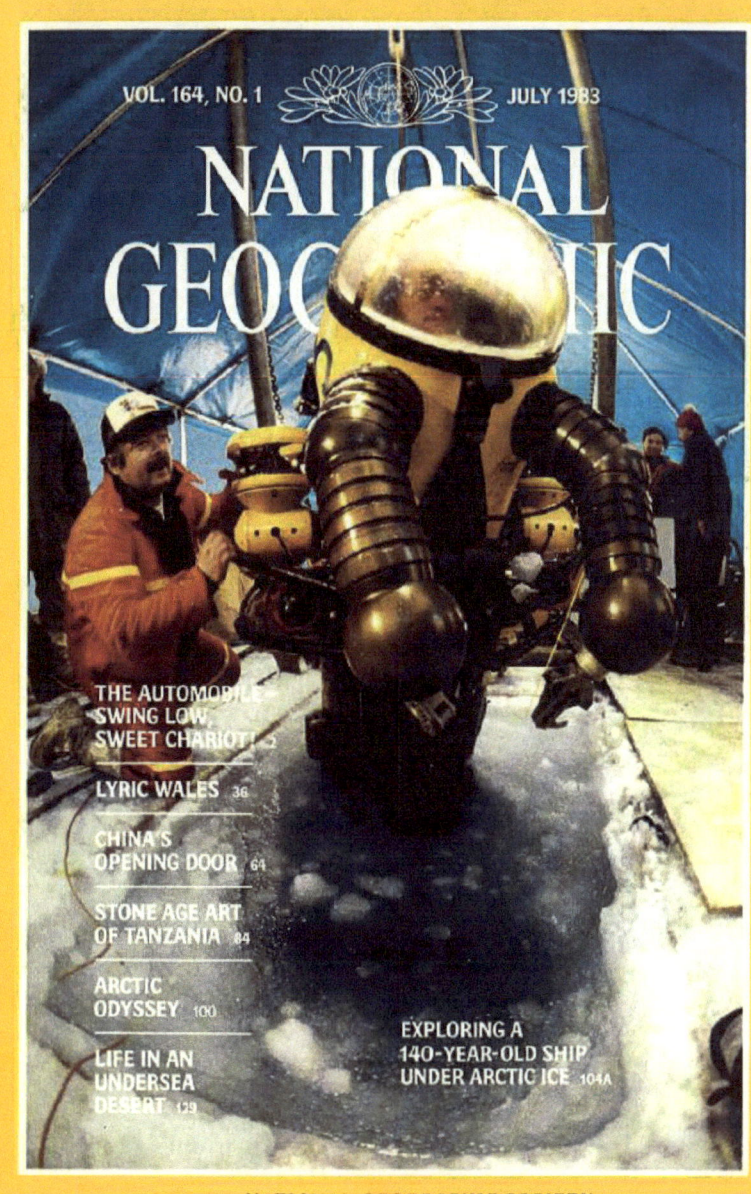

Phil Nuytten wearing an atmospheric diving suit on front cover of National Geographic VOL. 164 No.1 July 1983, photograph courtesy of the Nuytten family

Phil Nuytten at age of 12, showing his photography. photograph courtesy of the Nuytten family

Born in Vancouver in 1941, Phil developed an early interest in both diving and Northwest Coast Indigenous art. His entrepreneurial interests were supported by his parents, who backed him in early carving and diving endeavors.

Phil turned these passions into a successful career and sat on award and grant committees for several philanthropic diving and Indigenous organizations, as well as mentoring and supporting young ocean advocates and students. He received honorary doctorates from Queens University, Vancouver Island University, and Simon Fraser University.

His Excellency the Right Honourable David Johnston, 28th Governor General of Canada (2010-2017) presented the Officer insignia of the Order of Canada to Phil Nuytten, Photograph credit MCpl Vincent Carbonneau, Rideau Hall © OSGG, 2017, courtesy of the Nuytten family

In 1992, Phil received the Order of British Columbia in recognition of his contribution to the economic well-being of the province, his support of the indigenous culture, and for making the province known beyond its borders as a leader in underwater high-technology.

He was appointed an Officer of the Order of Canada in 2016 for his innovations in deep sea exploration. He was married to his high school sweetheart and beloved wife Mary for 58 years until her death in 2021. He continued to work, produce and collect until his death at the age of 81.

Phil Nuytten 1957, photograph courtesy of the Nuytten family

Phil began diving at the age of 11. He was a passionate activist for ocean health, dedicating his career to deep ocean work and exploration, and specifically to ensuring that divers have full access to continental shelf depths without the hazards of decompression.

He is widely regarded as one of the pioneers of the modern commercial diving industry and a significant force in the creation of new subsea technology.

He founded Western Canada's first diving shop at the age of 15, and two years later was one of the first divers in the water when the Iron Worker's Memorial Bridge collapsed.

He began a career in commercial diving and worked in logging camps and pulp mills before landing a diving job at the Bennett Dam on the Peace River. He founded Can-Dive Services Ltd in 1965, and co-founded Oceaneering International Inc., which became one of the largest underwater-skills companies in the world.

Phil Nuytten original 'Newtsuit' ADS (one-atmosphere diving suit) - photograph credit to Larry Goldstein, courtesy of the Nuytten family

Phil Nuytten 'Newtsuit', photograph courtesy of the Nuytten family

His work with high-Arctic expeditions, testing designs of life-support gear for use in polar and subpolar conditions, and his involvement in underwater activities in virtually all the world's oceans made Phil a leader in subsea technology.

In 1982 he patented a break-through rotary joint design, the basis for his world-famous 'Newtsuit' ADS (one-atmosphere diving suit). This led to its successor, the ultra-lightweight hard 'Exosuit ADS', which is a valuable tool for research scientists, commercial divers, military organizations and explorers globally.

His 'Remora' submarine rescue system is described as a major break-through in submarine safety, and his work on the 'DeepWorker' micro-subs to study deep ocean environmental impact has significantly increased scientists' understanding of underwater ecology, habitats and biodiversity.

Phil Nuytten wearing heavy gear 1959, photograph courtesy of the Nuytten family

He has appeared on the cover of dozens of publications, was a popular speaker, and published numerous technical papers on his leading-edge work. He was heavily involved in TV and film productions, consulting and providing submersibles and subsea devices for blockbuster movies such as James Cameron's 'The Abyss' and 'Titanic'. He also worked extensively with National Geographic, NASA and the Canadian Space Agency.

Phil Nuytten refurbishing Ellen Neel pole, photograph courtesy of the Nuytten family

Growing up in Vancouver's West side, Phil developed an interest in Northwest Coast art from studying the totem poles in Stanley Park and visiting the Vancouver Museum. At the age of 11 he learned of his Aboriginal heritage on his father's side, which fueled his interest in studying and learning the fundamentals of Northwest Coast carving.

He contacted noted Kwakwaka'wakw carver Ellen Neel, who agreed to give Phil lessons alongside her own children. He subsequently met other artists such as Mungo Martin and Amos Dawson, who would both have a profound influence on his life.

Phil was a talented artist in many media including drawing and painting, wood carving, and engraving. His vast collection includes not only impressive and rare examples of Charlie James, Ellen Neel and Mungo Martin works, but also early 19th century to modern day works by artists including Robert Davidson, Beau Dick, John Livingston, Doug Cranmer, Don Smith (Lelooska), Bill Reid, Joe and Willie Seaweed, Dorothy Grant, Henry Hunt, and others.

Dedicated to the preservation of Northwest Coast culture, Phil produced replicas of many early pieces, often working from early drawings and carvings. He was formally adopted by the Dawson family, who were Mamalilikulla from Village Island, and was given his first name Tlax'wsam (pronounced "Tlocksum"), meaning red snapper. In 1982 Phil published the seminal book on master carvers Charlie James, Ellen Neel and Mungo Martin, titled 'The Totem Carvers'.

Phil Nuytten centre-1995 potlatch he hosted in Alert Bay BC, photograph courtesy of the Nuytten family

Photograph courtesy of Uno Langmann Fine Art

PORTRAIT MASK WITH COPPER
unsigned, inset with hair and copper,
has been danced
PHIL NUYTTEN (Kah-Sah-Las)
(Canadian 1941-2023)
Provenance: Phil Nuytten Collection (2234)
Dimension in inches: 11 (H) x 8 (W) x 7 (D)

Copper eyebrows and eyes, photograph courtesy of
Uno Langmann Fine Art

In the Pacific Northwest, masks are central to the potlatch, a ceremonial feast with deep social and economic importance. During these gatherings, masks are used in dances and dramatic performances that narrate myths, spiritual beliefs, ancestral stories and social values.

Bentwood bowls are a distinctive and traditional form of craftsmanship among the indigenous peoples of the Pacific Northwest, particularly admired for their technical and aesthetic qualities. These bowls are made from a single piece of wood, usually cedar, which is steamed and bent into shape.

The technique involves cutting a single plank from a tree, making kerf cuts where the corners will be, and then bending the wood into a seamless, four-cornered shape. The joints are then pegged or stitched together, often with the roots of spruce trees or other natural materials.

BENTWOOD BOWL AND PESTLE
PHIL NUYTTEN (Kah-Sah-Las)
(Canadian 1941-2023)
bentwood/kerfed and carved and stained bowl, copy of one in the UBC Museum of Anthropology, with dark stain, together with wooden pestle in matching stain, pestle size 11 1/2" (L)
Provenance: Nuytten Collection
(2221+2)
Dimension in inches:
5 (H) x 9 (W) x 9 (D)

Photograph courtesy of Uno Langmann Fine Art

These bowls were not merely utilitarian items; they were integral to daily life and ceremonial use. Larger bentwood boxes and bowls were used to store food, clothing and valuables, while smaller ones could be used for serving food or during potlatch ceremonies.

The pestle, typically used in conjunction with a mortar (a larger and more robust bowl), is another crucial tool in indigenous kitchens. It was used for grinding and mashing food items, such as herbs, nuts and berries. The pestle would be crafted to fit comfortably in the hand and durable enough to withstand repeated use.

Photograph courtesy of Uno Langmann Fine Art

THUNDERBIRD AND WHALE
TOTEM POLE
Carved and painted wooden
totem pole of Thunderbird and
Whale.
Signed and dated on back "Phil
Nuytten 1988"
PHIL NUYTTEN
(Kah-Sah-Las)
(Canadian 1941-2023)
Dimension with base in inches:
20 ¼ (H) x 12 ¼ (W) x 8 ¼ (D)
Provenance:
Nuytten Collection (2209)

The thunderbird is a powerful supernatural creature in the mythology of many Northwest Coast tribes. It is often depicted as a gigantic bird capable of creating thunder by flapping its wings and lightning by blinking its eyes. The thunderbird represents strength, leadership, and protection.

SILVER ORCA BRACELET
silver bracelet signed on back "MA'EE'NUHK (ORCA) BY CHIEF MAHKWA (Phil Nuytten)"
PHIL NUYTTEN
(Kah-Sah-Las)
(Canadian 1941-2023)
Provenance:
Nuytten Collection
Dimension in inches: 2 (H)

Photograph courtesy of Uno Langmann Fine Art

The whale, usually a representation of an orca in Northwest Coast art, is revered for its size and strength. In many stories, the whale symbolizes emotional depth, family bonds, intelligence and communication. Some tribes believe the whale carries the history of the earth on its back and is a guardian of the sea and its creatures.

Photograph courtesy of Uno Langmann Fine Art

Framed photograph of Charlie James (left) and Mungo Martin with Thunderbird totem and Cedar mat, circa: 1930

The photo is described in 'The Totem Carvers', page 79:Plate '103': Charlie James (left) and Mungo Martin (with moustache). Ellen Neel described this
photograph to Marius Barbeau as another photo of (Charlie James)...with Mungo Martin. Behind them, a Thunderbird which he (C.J.) made for a grave at Alert Bay. In front, a cedar mat with a painting of a 'Sisiutl and a copper' - no date given, but probably around 1915. (Alert Bay, B.C. Photo: Courtesy City Archives, Vancouver IN-P-121.)

Charlie James, also known by his Kwakwaka'wakw name Yakuglas ('always giving things away'), was a legendary Northwest Coast Indigenous artist known for his masterful woodcarvings, particularly totem poles, masks and paintings. Born around 1867 in Port Townsend, Washington, US, he played a significant role in the preservation and continuation of Kwakwaka'wakw art and culture.

Mungo Martin, or Nakapenkem ('ten times over' Kwakwaka'wakw), was a pivotal figure in the revival and preservation of Pacific Northwest Coast Native art, particularly among the Kwakwaka'wakw people. Born in 1879 in Fort Rupert BC, Mungo Martin became renowned not only as a master carver but also as a keeper of his culture's traditions, songs and dances.

Mungo Martin also painted many of his carvings in the vibrant colors traditional to Kwakwaka'wakw art. His talents were not limited to woodcarving: Mungo Martin was also a respected singer and ceremonial dancer.

Charlie James was stepfather and mentor of Mungo Martin, and grandfather of Ellen Neel. Both were well-known Kwakwaka'wakw artists. The most widely viewed totem poles by Charlie James are a pair of Thunderbird house posts and a tall memorial pole of 'Sisaxo'las', at Stanley Park, Vancouver BC, Canada.

In 1952, Mungo Martin was appointed as the first official carver for the BC Provincial Museum in Victoria. He built the museum's first outdoor totem pole park, where he restored old poles and created new ones.

He composed many songs and dances, which he performed at potlatches and other ceremonial gatherings, further cementing his role as a cultural custodian.

Photograph courtesy of Uno Langmann Fine Art

Cedar mat painted with a Sisiutl and copper, circa: 1915
CHARLIE JAMES (YAKUGLAS)
(Kwakwaka'wakw (Kwakiutl)
Circa 1867-1938)
Provenance: Nuytten Collection (2058)
Dimension in inches: 38 ½ (H) x 73 (W),
With frame: 45 ½ (H) x 80 (W)

Thunderbird totem, circa: 1915
CHARLIE JAMES (YAKUGLAS)
(Kwakwaka'wakw (Kwakiutl) Circa 1867-1938)
Provenance: Nuytten Collection (2058)
Dimension in inches: 31 (H) x 52 (W) x 8 (D)

Photograph courtesy of Uno Langmann Fine Art

HENRY HUNT (MU-BIN-KIM)
(Kwakwaka'wakw (Kwakiutl)
1923-1985

The Kwakiutl artist Henry Hunt was born in Fort Rupert, Vancouver Island, BC. He began as a part time carver in 1954 at the BC Provincial Museum and became chief carver in 1962 after the death of Mungo Martin. He worked with the Museum until 1974, much of the time spent carving totem poles with his mentor Mungo Martin and later with his eldest son Tony Hunt.

He carved both for traditional ceremonial use as well as for sale. Henry Hunt is revered as a totem carver, designer and carver of monumental Kwakwaka'wakw (Kwakiutl) sculpture. In 1970-71, Henry Hunt along with his son Tony Hunt carved a memorial 35-foot totem pole to Mungo Martin, the first pole to be erected in the Alert Bay graveyard in many years.

In the early 1960's Henry Hunt was approached by a ceramic crafts company and was encouraged to carve masks, dishes, poles, pins, buttons, etc, all of which were cast and sold widely as tourist items. Some of the products were painted in traditional Kwakwaka'wakw (Kwakiutl) manner by Henry's wife Helen but by far the majority of the output was glazed in single colours. These pieces have since become quite collectible. The moulds were eventually sold and production ceased in the late 1960's. The collection featured totem poles, ceremonial masks, feast dishes, bowls, wall planters, salt and pepper shakers, ashtrays, miniature jewellery and bookends. There was a choice of fifteen colors for the glazed pieces; the jewellery items (earrings, brooches, cufflinks, tie bars and bolo ties) produced in porcelain had a choice of eight colors.

Photograph courtesy of Uno Langmann Fine Art

KILLER WHALE FEAST BOWL
HENRY HUNT (MU-BIN-KIM) (Kwakwaka'wakw (Kwakiutl) 1923-1985)

Wooden feast bowl in the form of a killer whale with bird head as a dorsal fin lid, and bear head as tail, unpainted, signed on bottom "Hunt Kwagiulth Killer Whale Feast Bowl"
Provenance: Nuytten Collection (2410)
Dimension in inches: 10 (H) x 24 (W) x 7 (D)

EAGLE SPOON
ROBERT CHARLES (GUUD SAN GLANS) DAVIDSON (Haida/Canadian born 1946)

Photograph courtesy of Uno Langmann Fine Art

Silver spoon with engraved eagle motif, inscribed "Davidson 71"
Provenance: Nuytten Collection (3075)
Dimension in inches: 5.75 (H) x 1.75 (W) x 0.3 (D)

Robert Charles Davidson, Guud San Glans ('Eagle of the Dawn') of the Eagle Clan, was born in Hydaburg, Alaska in 1946 and was raised in Old Massett, Haida Gwaii. His father, Claude Davidson, and Grandfather, Claude Davidson Sr., began Robert's carving career in wood and argillite when he was 13 years old. He was strongly influenced by his great-grandfather Charles Edenshaw and his grandmother Florence Davidson who had 13 children, providing a large number of 'aunties' to whom Robert was very close.

It was necessary to move to Vancouver in 1965 for Robert to complete high school, and it was there that he learned to produce silkscreen prints. In 1966 he was demonstrating carving at Eaton's Department Store where he met Bill Reid, with whom he would develop a lasting relationship.

Robert moved into Bill Reid's studio where he apprenticed under him for the next eighteen months. Robert made his own tools and would learn the fundamentals of two-dimensional design. In 1967 he attended the Vancouver School of Art (now Emily Carr University) and was swept up in the 1960's abstract and modern art scene. He enrolled in a jewellery course where he began experimenting with abstraction, which also influenced his print making. He taught for six months in 1968 at 'Ksan, a reconstructed village near Hazelton, and in 1969 he returned to Masset where he carved and erected a forty-foot totem pole, the first to be raised in Haida Gwaii in almost a hundred years.

Widely recognized, Robert Davidson has won many awards including the Governor General's Award for Visual Arts and the Audain Prize for Lifetime Achievement Award in the Visual Arts. He is the recipient of the Order of BC and the Order of Canada, and is the subject of the documentary Haida Modern.

The Vancouver Art Gallery has held nearly twenty-five solo shows of Robert Davidson's work, and his carvings, prints, paintings and jewelry can be found in major collections and institutions worldwide.

Original painting, in black, green and red, signed on lower right 'Robert Davidson 1995', this is the painting reference for the serigraph 'Getting Ready to Take Flight' 1995, edition of 72 (print not included).

Photograph courtesy of Uno Langmann Fine Art

Accompanied by a personal letter from the artist: 'Phil Nuytten: For your continued interest in my work...The painting is the beginning of the next part of my life. Sincerely, Robert Davidson'.

'GETTING READY TO TAKE FLIGHT'
ROBERT CHARLES (GUUD SAN GLANS) DAVIDSON
(Haida/Canadian born 1946)
Provenance: Nuytten Collection (2701)
Dimension in inches: 42 (H) x 29.5 (W)

CARVED WOOD TOTEM

Unpainted wood totem, the back hollowed out, inscribed on back "384/137112 Alaska Bought by Mother 1897", with Sotheby's tag from sale November 8, 1977 described as "Tlingit wood totem, unpainted, in the form of a seated bear surmounted on the figure of 'the strong man of the sea' standing atop a fish with the fins to either side, the figure naturalistically portrayed with strongly pronounced facial features, wearing a clow crown-like headdress", possibly American Haida (Kaigani), second half of the 19th century

Provenance: Nuytten Collection (3107)
Sotheby's November 8, 1977 lot 38
Dimension in inches: 26.25 (H) x 4.5 (W) x 3.75 (D)

Photograph courtesy of Uno Langmann Fine Art

Author: JEANETTE LANGMANN

Jeanette Langmann has spent her life in the arts. Daughter of Uno Langmann, a respected international authority on art and antiques, Jeanette has acquired over 30 years of experience working in the field. She studied at the University of British Columbia before becoming a second generation art dealer and appraiser in the family business.

Jeanette is an active member of the professional antiques and fine arts community both locally and internationally and travels worldwide to research and collect fine and decorative arts. She has a particular interest in historical Canadian art from the 19th and early 20th century. She is an expert on CBC's Canadian Antiques Roadshow, a past President of the Art Dealers Association of Canada and advises as Chair of the ADAC's Appraisals Committee as well as to the Canadian Personal Property Export Review Board in Ottawa. She sits on the board of the South Granville Business Improvement Association, South Granville Gallery Association and is a past board member of the Vancouver Archives, Antique Dealers Association of Canada, and the Greater Vancouver Antique Dealers Association.

Established in 1967, Uno Langmann Fine Art is Canada's foremost specialist in the finest quality European and North American paintings and antiques from the 18th, 19th and early 20th centuries.

With over 50 years in business, the gallery assists clients in assembling important collections and sourcing quality artwork, works closely with museums and institutions and endeavors to keep major works within Canada.

Photographs courtesy of Uno Langmann Fine Art

菲尔·纽顿（1941-2023）是许多领域的先驱：水下探险家、海底工程师、发明家、海洋考古学家、企业家、曲作者、雕刻家、作家、原住民文化倡导者和收藏家。

博学和涉猎广泛，使他常被称为"文艺复兴时代的人"。

《国家地理杂志》在'探索深域'中描述道："菲尔是一位富有创造力的工程师，他的商业潜水记录令人印象深刻，结合艺术家和专业魔术师的才干，菲尔的幽默感可以解除任何人的武装"。

加拿大著名水下探险家约瑟夫·麦克尼斯博士在其著作《布雷多尔巴恩的故事》中表示，"菲尔是那些非凡的人物之一，由于他广泛的技能和知识，他似乎是从另一个世纪浮现出来的"。

1941年菲尔·纽顿出生于加拿大温哥华，很早就对潜水和原住民艺术产生了浓厚兴趣。

父母发现他的企业家天赋并支持他从小学习雕刻和潜水。之后菲尔将兴趣转为成功的职业生涯，并担任多个慈善潜水和原住民组织的委员会成员，指导和支持年轻人学习原住民艺术和海洋生态保护。

他先后获得了皇后大学、温哥华岛大学和西蒙弗雷泽大学的荣誉博士学位。

1992年，菲尔获得了不列颠哥伦比亚省勋章，以表彰他对该省经济和福祉的贡献，及对原住民文化的长期支持和推广。菲尔的杰出技术贡献，使该省作为水下高科技领域的领导者而闻名海外。

2016年，他因在深海探索的创新而被授予加拿大勋章。

菲尔与高中时期的恋人、深爱的妻子玛丽结婚58年。在玛丽于2021年去世后，他继续工作和收藏，直到81岁去世。

从11岁开始潜水，菲尔是一位热衷于海洋生态保护的活动家。他将自己的职业生涯都奉献给深海科技和探索工作。

他的发明使潜水员能够完全进入大陆架深处而不会面临减压造成的危险。

菲尔被认为是现代商业潜水行业的先驱和深海技术创新的推动力量。

來自"文藝復興時代"的收藏家

— 珍妮特·朗曼

在15岁时，菲尔创立了加拿大西部第一家潜水店。

两年后，当钢铁工人纪念桥倒塌时，他成为了第一批下水救援的潜水员。

他的职业生涯始于商业潜水，起先他在伐木场和纸浆厂工作，然后在皮斯河的贝内特大坝获得了一份潜水工作。

1965年，菲尔21岁时，创立了Can-Dive Services Ltd，并与他人共同创立了Oceaneering International Inc.，之后该公司成为世界上最大的水下技术公司之一。

他参于了北极高纬度探险和用于极地条件下使用的生命支持装备的设计测试。

广泛涉及几乎世界上所有海洋的水下活动，使菲尔成为潜水技术的领导者。

1982年，他发明了旋转接头设计专利，是重大的潜水技术突破，也是他举世闻名的"单气压潜水服"（Newtsuit ADS）的基础，并进一步催生了其后继产品—"超轻量/硬质潜水服"（Exosuit ADS）。

该潜水服是全球海洋研究科学家、商业潜水员、军事组织和探险家的宝贵工具。

菲尔的另一个发明"Remora潜艇救援系统"，被形容为"潜艇安全方面的创新突破"。

他驾驶"DeepWorker"微型潜艇，对深海环境进行的研究，极大帮助了科学家了解水下生态、栖息地和生物多样性。

菲尔曾出现在数十种出版物的封面上，是位广受欢迎的演讲者，并发表了大量关于其前沿工作的技术论文。

他积极参与电视和电影制作，为詹姆斯·卡梅隆的《深渊》和《泰坦尼克号》等大片提供潜水器和海底设备的咨询和服务。他还与国家地理杂志、美国宇航局和加拿大航天局广泛合作。

成长于温哥华西区，菲尔通过研究斯坦利公园的图腾柱和参观温哥华博物馆，对原住民艺术产生了浓厚兴趣。

11岁时了解到自己源于父亲的原住民血缘，激发了他对西北岸原住民雕刻技艺的学习和研究。

他联系了著名的 Kwakwaka'wakw 族原住民雕刻家爱伦·尼尔，后者同意给菲尔和她自己的孩子一起上雕刻课。

随后，他遇到了蒙戈·马丁和阿莫斯·道森等其他艺术家，他们对菲尔产生了深远影响。

菲尔致力于保护西北岸原住民文化，制作了许多早期作品的复制品。

他被来自乡村岛Mamalilikulla族的道森家族正式收养，并赋予他原住民名字'Ilax'wsam'，意思是红鲷鱼。

1982年，菲尔出版了介绍雕刻大师查理·詹姆斯（Charlie James）、爱伦·尼尔（Ellen Neel）和蒙戈·马丁（Mungo Martin）的著作《图腾雕刻家》。该书对原住民艺术推广影响深远。

作为一位才华横溢的艺术家，菲尔擅长绘画、木雕和雕刻。

他的藏品不仅包括查理·詹姆斯、爱伦·尼尔和蒙戈·马丁令人印象深刻且罕见的作品，还包括罗伯特·戴维森、博·迪克、约翰·利文斯顿、道格·克兰默、唐·史密斯、比尔·里德、乔威利·西韦德、多罗西·格兰特、亨利·亨特等艺术家从19世纪早期到现代的作品。

菲尔·纽顿（加拿大 1941-2023）
原住民仪式面具
镶嵌头发和铜，
曾于重要仪式舞蹈中使用
来源：菲尔·纽顿收藏 (2234)
规格(厘米)：28(高) x 20(宽) x 18(深)

在太平洋西北地区，仪式面具是飨宴仪式的核心道具。飨宴仪式在原住民生活中有深远社会和经济意义，部落成员聚集一堂，庆祝重要场合如新生，成人礼，婚礼及纪念重大事件。

在这些聚会期间，仪式面具被用于舞蹈和戏剧表演，讲述神话、精神信仰、祖先故事和部落社会的价值。

银质虎鲸手镯
银质手镯，雕刻虎鲸图纹
背面签名 "MA'EE'NUHK (虎鲸) BY CHIEF MANKWA"
(菲尔·纽顿的酋长名)
来源：菲尔·纽顿收藏
规格(厘米)：5 (高)

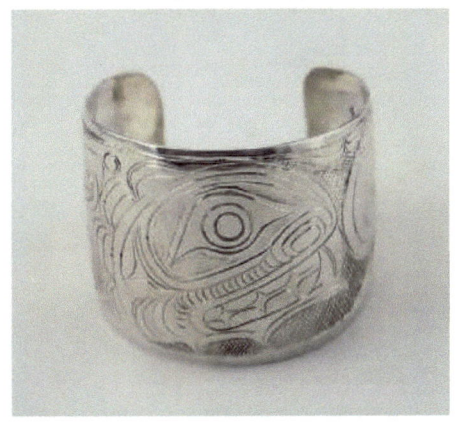

菲尔·纽顿（加拿大 1941-2023）
弯木碗和木杵
木碗，弯木/锯痕工艺、雕刻和染色工艺，
按UBC人类学博物馆展品中，一个深色染色的木碗复制，附配套木杵，同一深色染色
来源：菲尔·纽顿收藏 (2221+2)
碗规格 (厘米): 12.7(高) x 22.9(宽) x 22.9(长)
杵规格 (厘米): 29.2(长)

弯木碗是太平洋西北部原住民的一种独特的传统工艺，因其技术和美学品质而受到特别推崇。这些碗由一块木头（通常是雪松）制成，经过独特的蒸煮和弯曲而成型。

该技术包括从树上切割一块木板，在拐角处进行切口切割，然后将木材弯曲成无缝的四角形状。通常再用云杉树根或其他天然材料将接合部固定或缝合在一起。

这些碗是日常生活和仪式用途不可或缺的一部分。较大的曲木盒子和碗用于存放食物、衣服和贵重物品，而较小的则可用于盛放食物或在飨宴仪式上使用。

杵通常与研钵（一种更大、更坚固的碗）结合使用，是当地厨房的另一个重要工具。它用于研磨和捣碎食品，如香草、坚果和浆果。杵的设计要舒适，并且足够耐用，以承受大量重复使用。

雷鸟是许多西北海岸部落神话中一种强大的超自然生物。它经常被描绘成一只巨大的鸟，能够通过拍打翅膀产生雷霆，通过眨眼产生闪电。雷鸟代表力量、领导力和守护。

在西北岸原住民艺术中鲸鱼通常代表虎鲸（亦名逆戟鲸），因其体型和力量而受到尊敬。在许多故事中，鲸鱼象征着深度的情感、家庭的纽带、智慧和沟通。一些部落相信鲸鱼的背上承载着地球的历史，是海洋及其生物的守护者。

菲尔·纽顿（加拿大 1941-2023）
雷鸟和鲸鱼图腾柱
木制图腾柱，
雕刻和彩绘成雷鸟和鲸鱼图纹
背面有作者签名并注明日期 "Phil Nuytten 1988"
来源：菲尔·纽顿收藏 (2209)
带底座规格 (厘米)：
52(高) x 31(宽) x 29 (长)

查理·詹姆斯（约 1867 年-1938 年）
雷鸟图腾柱
年代：约 1915 年
来源：菲尔·纽顿收藏 (2058)
规格(厘米)：78.8(高) x 132(宽) x 20.3(深)

查理·詹姆斯和蒙戈·马丁镶框照片，查理·詹姆斯和蒙戈·马丁手举雪松挂毯，背后为雷鸟图腾柱，不列颠哥伦比亚省阿勒特湾。照片来源：温哥华城市档案馆。IN-P-121

在菲尔·纽顿《图腾雕刻者》第79页描述这张照片："103图：查理·詹姆斯（左）和蒙戈·马丁（留着小胡子）。爱伦·尼尔向马吕斯·巴博描述到这是又一张（查理·詹姆斯）照片……和蒙戈·马丁。在他们身后，有一个他制作的雷鸟图腾柱。前面有一张雪松挂毯，上面有"双头海蛇"和"铜"的绘画，没有给出日期，约为1915年。"

查理·詹姆斯（Charlie James），以他的Kwakwaka'wakw族名字"总是馈赠礼物"而闻名。他是位传奇的西北岸原住民艺术家，以精湛的雕刻，尤其是图腾柱、面具和绘画而闻名。他于1867年左右出生于美国华盛顿州汤森港，在保护和延续Kwakwaka'wakw原住民艺术和文化方面发挥了重要作用。

查理·詹姆斯是蒙戈·马丁的继父和导师，也是爱伦·尼尔的外祖父。两人也均为著名的Kwakwaka'wakw族艺术家。位于温哥华斯坦利公园，他的一对雷鸟屋和"Sisaxo'las"纪念图腾柱最广为人知。

蒙戈·马丁（Mungo Martin），Kwakwaka'wakw族名字"十倍的"，是太平洋西北岸原住民艺术复兴和保护的关键人物。他于1879年出生于不列颠哥伦比亚省鲁珀特堡，不仅作为雕刻大师而闻名，而且是其文化传统、歌曲和舞蹈的守护者。

1952年，蒙戈·马丁被任命为位于维多利亚市，不列颠哥伦比亚省博物馆的第一位官方雕刻师。他建造了博物馆的第一个户外图腾柱公园，在那里他修复了旧的图腾柱并制作了新的图腾柱。

他还用 Kwakwaka'wakw 传统艺术的鲜艳色彩绘制了许多雕刻作品。蒙戈·马丁的才华不仅限于木雕，也是一位受人尊敬的歌手和礼仪舞者。他创作了许多原住民歌曲和舞蹈，并在飨宴和其他仪式聚会上表演，进一步确立了他作为原住民文化守护者的崇高地位。

查理·詹姆斯（约1867年-1938年）
雪松挂毯
绘有双头海蛇和铜，双头海蛇是超自然的生灵，也是Kwakwaka'wakw族的族徽，铜代表财富
年代：约1915年
来源：菲尔·纽顿收藏（2058）
规格（厘米）：97.8（高）x 185.4（宽）

亨利·亨特（MU-BIN-KIM）(Kwakwaka'wakw，1923-1985)
虎鲸盛宴碗
木质，椭圆碗雕刻成虎鲸形状，背鳍盖雕刻成雷鸟头，虎鲸尾部雕刻成熊头，未上漆
底部签名 "Hunt Kwagiulth Killer Whale Feast Bowl（狩猎卡吉乌斯虎鲸飨宴碗）"
来源：菲尔·纽顿收藏 (2410)
规格（厘米）: 25.4（高）x 17.8（宽）x 61(长)

亨利·亨特出生于不列颠哥伦比亚省温哥华岛的鲁珀特堡。1954年他在BC省博物馆担任兼职雕刻师，并于1962年蒙戈·马丁去世后成为首席雕刻师。在博物馆工作到1974年，他大部分时间都与导师蒙戈·马丁（Mungo Martin）以及与长子托尼·亨特（Tony Hunt）一起雕刻图腾柱。亨利·亨特的雕刻既用于传统仪式，也用于出售。1970-71年亨利·亨特和他的儿子托尼·亨特为蒙戈·马丁雕刻了一根35英尺高的图腾柱，这是多年来在阿勒湾竖立的第一根图腾柱。

1960一家陶瓷工艺品公司邀请他雕刻面具、盘子、杆子、别针、纽扣等，所有这些都被铸造并作为旅游纪念品出售。一些产品由亨利的妻子海伦以传统方式绘制。这些纪念品变得非常具有收藏价值，制作模具也最终被出售，并于六十年代末停止生产。该系列包括图腾柱、仪式面具、盛宴碗、墙壁花盆、盐罐、胡椒瓶、烟灰缸、微型珠宝和书立。釉面有十五种颜色可供选择，用瓷器制作的珠宝首饰（耳环、胸针、袖扣、领带夹和领带）有八种颜色可供选择。

罗伯特·查尔斯·戴维森（Robert Charles Davidson），原住民海达族，鹰部落的黎明之鹰家族（Guud San Glans），1946年出生于阿拉斯加州海达堡，在海达瓜伊的老马塞特长大。

在父亲克劳德·戴维森（Claude Davidson）和祖父老克劳德·戴维森（Claude Davidson Sr.）指导下，罗伯特13岁时就开始了木和泥岩雕刻生涯。他深受曾祖父查尔斯·伊登肖（Charles Edenshaw）和祖母弗洛伦斯·戴维森（Florence Davidson）的影响。祖母有13个孩子，使罗伯特有很多与他关系密切的"阿姨"。

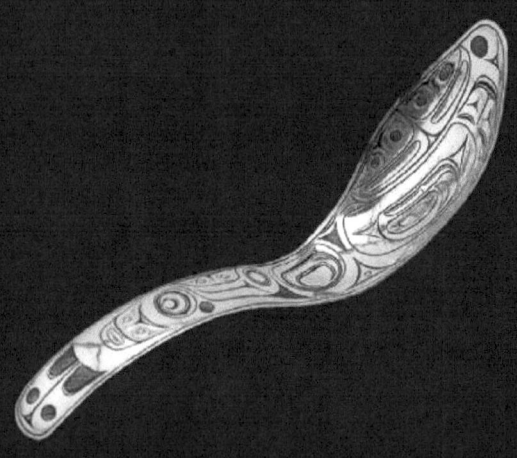

银勺
罗伯特·查尔斯·戴维森(GUUD SAN GLANS) （Haida/加拿大人，1946-）
银质，雕刻鹰图案，并刻有签名"Davidson 71"
来源：菲尔·纽顿收藏(3075)
规格（厘米）：0.8(高) x 4.5(宽) x 14.6(长)

1965年罗伯特搬到温哥华完成高中学业，在那里他学会了制作丝网印刷品。1966年他在伊顿百货公司展示雕刻作品，在那里认识了比尔·里德（Bill Reid），并与他建立了持久的关系。罗伯特搬进了比尔·里德的工作室，在接下来的十八个月里跟随里德当学徒。罗伯特制作了自己的工具，并学习了二维设计的基础知识。

1967年他就读于温哥华艺术学院（现为艾米丽·卡尔大学），并被抽象和现代艺术圈所吸引。他参加了珠宝课程，在那里他开始尝试抽象艺术，这也影响了他的版画创作。1968年他在黑兹尔顿（Hazelton）附近重建的村庄'卡山'教了六个月的书，1969年他回到老马塞特，在那里雕刻并竖起一根40英尺高的图腾柱，这是近一百年来海达瓜伊（Haida Gwaii）竖起的第一根图腾柱。

在此期间他的名声传开经常被委托制作图腾、面具、版画以及金银珠宝。罗伯特·戴维森因其对传统海达雕塑和设计的透彻理解及掌握而闻名。他赢得许多奖项，包括总督视觉艺术奖和奥丹视觉艺术终身成就奖。

他是不列颠哥伦比亚省勋章和加拿大勋章的获得者，也是纪录片《现代海达》的主角。温哥华美术馆已举办近二十五场罗伯特·戴维森的作品个展，他的雕刻品、版画、绘画和珠宝作品在世界各地的主要收藏机构中都能找到。

罗伯特·查尔斯·戴维森
(GUUD SAN GLANS)（原住民海达族/加拿大，1946年- ）
"准备起飞"
绘画，配色黑、绿、红，
右下签名 "Robert Davidson 1995"
年代：1995
来源：菲尔·纽顿收藏 (2701)
规格 (厘米)：106.7(高) x 75(宽)

这是丝网版画《准备起飞》的原作，
附有艺术家的一封私人信件："菲尔·纽顿：
您对我的作品一直持续感兴趣。我很高兴你收到了这幅画和毯子。这幅画是我人生下一篇章的开始。此致，罗伯特·戴维森"。

木雕图腾

未上漆，木质，背面镂空，背面刻字"384/137112 阿拉斯加，由母亲 1897 年购买"，1977 年 11 月 8 日在苏富比拍卖而得附苏富比标签，拍品描述"特林吉特木图腾，未上漆，坐着的熊位于底部，顶端"海上力士"站于鱼上，鱼鳍展向双侧，人物描绘自然，面部神情夸张强烈，戴着类似皇冠的头饰"，可能年代十九世纪下半叶，美国海达族（Kaigani）

来源：苏富比 1977 年 11 月 8 日拍品 38，菲尔·纽顿收藏（3075）

规格（厘米）：66.7(高) x 11.5(宽) x 9.5(长)

作者：珍妮特·朗曼

珍妮特·朗曼（Jeanette Langmann）一生致力于艺术，是受人尊敬的国际艺术和古董权威 乌诺·朗曼的女儿，拥有30多年的古董行业经验。她曾就读于不列颠哥伦比亚大学，之后成为艺术品评估师和家族企业的第二代经营者。

作为本地和国际古董界及美术界的活跃成员，珍妮特旅行世界各地，研究和收集美术及装饰艺术，对19世纪和20世纪初的加拿大艺术有浓厚兴趣。她是加拿大广播公司专栏节目-古董秀的专家、加拿大艺术品经销商协会前任主席，并担任加拿大艺术协会评估委员会主席以及渥太华加拿大个人财产出口审查委员会的顾问。

"乌诺·朗曼艺术"成立于1967年，是加拿大首屈一指的艺术品专家，主营18、19世纪和20世纪初最优质的欧洲和北美绘画和古董。该画廊协助客户收集重要藏品和艺术品，与博物馆、教研机构密切合作，并努力将重要艺术作品保留在加拿大境内。

本文照片均由"乌诺·朗曼艺术"和菲尔·纽顿家族提供

East meets West

-By Terry Sasaki

Terry Sasaki. Photograph courtesy of Sasaki Art Gallery

Art is an expression of yourself and a life you own. It can take many forms and methods. Ultimately it will create your lifestyle.

As a designer, fashion maker and inspirational painter, Terry Sasaki has created an 'East meets West', in line with his upbringing and sensibility.

Photograph courtesy of Sasaki Art Gallery

Tranquility
Rice paper collage
Acrylic on Canvas
TERRY SASAKI
Dimension in inch: 20 (H) x 20 (W)

The four seasons continue to play a major role in Japanese creativity. And again, Terry Sasaki exemplifies this creativity in his modern application of rice paper collage.

Sasaki's journey into the world of art began in Japan, where he was deeply influenced by traditional Japanese aesthetics and techniques, especially in the Heinan era (794-1185 CE), the golden age of Japanese civilization.

During the Heinan era, influenced by China, the Japanese developed their own culture based on an interpretation of the natural world around them.

A scene of the Chapter "TAKEKAWA"(Bamboo River) of Illustrated handscroll of Tale of Genji. The handscroll was made in Heinan period about 1130 CE and stored in TOKUGAWA Museum. Source:GENJI-MONOGATARI-EMAKI published by TOKUGAWA MUSEUM, NAGOYA, Japan, 1937. commons.wikimedia.org/wiki/File:Genji_emaki_TAKEKAWA.jpg

His early exposure to the delicate beauty of Washi paper and the intricate art of kiri-e (cut paper art), laid the foundation for his unique artistic voice. After moving to Canada, Sasaki immersed himself in Western artistic traditions, absorbing new techniques and perspectives that would later enrich his work.

Use of traditional Japanese rice paper provides a delicate and ethereal quality to his paintings. The paper, often used in Japanese calligraphy and sumi-e (ink painting), brings a sense of lightness to his work.

At the heart of Sasaki's paintings lies a captivating fusion of Eastern and Western cultures. He masterfully combines traditional Japanese materials like rice paper and kiri-e with modern acrylics on canvas, creating works that are both visually striking and texturally rich. This blending of materials and techniques results in a fascinating texture that draws viewers into a tactile and visual exploration of his art.

Kiri-e adds an intricate, almost sculptural element, where the paper is meticulously cut and layered, creating depth and dimensionality. The incorporation of acrylics introduces bold, vibrant colors and modernity, allowing Sasaki to experiment with strong visual contrasts and dynamic compositions.

Photograph courtesy of Sasaki Art Gallery

Gathering
Rice paper collage
Acrylic on Canvas
TERRY SASAKI
Dimension in inch: 24 (H) x 30(W)

The visual impact is undeniable in his paintings. Abstract forms and motifs of natural elements evoke the deep connection to nature—a common theme in Japanese art.

Western influences are evident in bold use of color and contemporary aesthetic sensibilities. This harmonious blend of styles creates a sense of universality, making his work resonate with a global audience.

Sasaki's paintings invite us to appreciate the richness of our shared cultural heritage and the endless possibilities that emerge when different artistic traditions come together. It is a beautiful reminder of the harmony and creativity that can be achieved through unity.

'A painting is there, people interpret in different ways. If it speaks to you, then it is a good painting for you.' Terry Sasaki

Photograph courtesy of Sasaki Art Gallery

Gathering
Rice paper collage
Acrylic on Canvas
TERRY SASAKI
Dimension in inch: 40 (H) x 30 (W)

Photograph courtesy of Sasaki Art Gallery

Waterfall
Rice paper collage
Acrylic on Canvas
TERRY SASAKI
Dimension in inch: 40 (H) x 30 (W)

Photographs courtesy of Sasaki Art Gallery

Wear-able Fashion Art

Blending Asian aesthetics
with stylish European cut
100% cotton
TERRY SASAKI

Feasts for the eyes and palate, Photographs courtesy of Sasaki Art Gallery

At home Terry enjoys growing flowers and cooking delicious dishes.

Gem Jewelry

Natural water pearls, turquoises, corals and precious stones, each one is finely selected to create a unique piece.

TERRY SASAKI

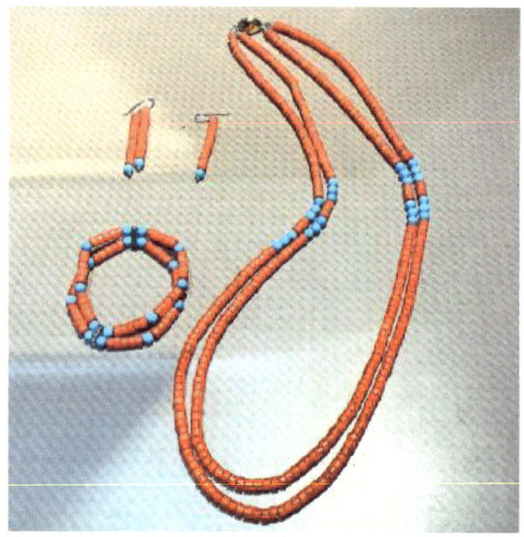

Photographs courtesy of Sasaki Art Gallery

Author: TERRY SASAKI

Terry Sasaki was born in Japan and has lived in Canada for more than 45 years. He works with both visual art and concepts towards developing an idea. From this creative flow emerges either an elaborate piece of jewelry, a comfortable yet fashionable line of clothing or a visually powerful art piece.

Sasaki's multifaceted personality has led him to an incursion not only into the art scene, but also into the fashion business world.

For over 36 years, Terry has successfully grown his own gallery at the Pan Pacific Hotel in Vancouver, produced exhibitions and fashion shows, traveled around the world and maintained a mind open to new and exciting ideas.

Photograph courtesy of Sasaki Art Gallery

Lotus
Kiri-e
TERRY SASAKI
Dimension in inch: 20 (H) x 20 (W)

東方會西方
- 特里·佐佐木

藝術是自我表達，也是生活。它形式多樣、手法豐富，最終它塑造了生活的方式。

作為一名畫家、時裝設計師和藝術家，特里·佐佐木 (Terry Sasaki) 創造了屬於他自己的風格「東方會西方」，這源於其成長經歷和感悟。

佐佐木的藝術之旅始於日本，他深受日本傳統美學和技藝的薰陶，特別是日本文化的黃金年代 - 平安時期（794-1185）的影響。

平安時期，中國唐朝對日本產生深遠影響。以此為基礎，日本人通過對周圍自然世界的詮釋，發展了自己的文化。

特里·佐佐木和他設計的時裝

他早期接觸到日本傳統手工造紙-和紙的精致之美和日本繁複的剪紙繪艺术，奠定了他独特的艺术表達基础。移居加拿大后，佐佐木沉浸於西方艺术传统，吸收新的技巧和观点，進一步丰富了藝術的表现。

佐佐木绘画的核心是东西方文化的融合。他巧妙地将日本传统和纸、剪纸绘藝術等与现代丙烯繪画相融合，创作出極具视觉冲击力又质感丰富的作品。这一融合产生了迷人的想像空間，吸引观众深入他的作品进行视觉和触觉探索。

日本传统和纸的使用为他的画作带来精致而空灵的品质。这种纸张经常用于日本书法和水墨画，使他的作品呈現獨特的轻盈感。

剪紙绘添加了繁複、近乎雕塑的元素，纸张经过精心切割和分层，创造出深度和维度。丙烯颜料带来了大胆、充满活力的色彩和现代感，使佐佐木能够尝试强烈的视觉对比和动态构图。

他的画作有无可否认的视觉冲击力。意喻四季的抽象图案象徵与大自然的深刻联系——這是日本艺术的常见主题。西方的影响在色彩的大胆运用和所表现的现代之美中显而易见，使他的作品引起来自全球不同地域藝術蒐藏家的共鳴。

佐佐木的作品邀请我们欣赏人類共同文化遗产的丰富性和不同艺术传统融合时所展现的无限可能性。它的美丽提醒我們，藝術的相互借鑑可以实现和谐及激發無盡创造。

"画就在那里，人们以不同的方式解读它。如果它能对你傾訴，那么这就是一幅屬於你的画。"
-特里·佐佐木

宁静
和纸剪紙，丙烯畫； 規格（英寸）：20（高）x 20（宽）
特里·佐佐木

四季在日本的藝術创作中舉足輕重。特里·佐佐木以和纸剪紙結合丙烯畫的運用，再次体現了日本藝術的创造力。

夏
和纸剪紙，丙烯畫
規格（英寸）：24（高）x 18（宽）
特里·佐佐木

生活就是藝術，
特里喜歡在家裡種植花卉和烹飪美味佳餚。

作者：特里·佐佐木

特里·佐佐木出生於日本，在加拿大生活超過45年。
他從事視覺藝術創作，並將概念發展為創意商品。從這一創意流程中誕生的，或是精緻的珠寶，或是舒適的時尚服裝系列，亦或是極具視覺衝擊力的畫作。

特里多面的個性使他不僅涉足藝術界，還成功地涉足時尚界。
已有36年歷史的佐佐木畫廊座落於溫哥華地標-泛太平洋酒店，成為來自世界各地商界、藝術界名流光顧之地。多年來，特里舉辦各類畫展、時尚秀、周遊世界並始終以開放的態度面對新的或是令人興奮的想法。

本文照片由佐佐木畫廊提供

佐佐木設計的時裝

The Recital of the Future

—By Scott Brooks

Young, talented, and ambitious performers from the classical field are demonstrating frustration with, and resistance to, the stuffier norms of earlier generations, and it's about time. When we consider the direction opera and vocal recitals are going, this concert is particularly illuminating. Considerable effort has been put into making the experience as thematically coherent as possible, and Orlinski exerts his presence as the central performer in order to impose upon the audience a clear interpretation of the music.

Last month I heard the countertenor Jakub Józef Orlinski perform his recital, Beyond, in collaboration with Il Pomo d'Oro, the Baroque specialist orchestra. The repertoire for the performance was drawn from Orlinski's eponymous album, also recorded with Il Pomo d'Oro, with a few adjustments.

Some of the performance elements he includes are intentionally, and strikingly, anachronistic, for example the series of break-dancing moves that represent the pain and anguish of a jilted lover. Most of his activities on stage would be considered violations of traditional codes of decorum, and this seems to be part of the point.

For we are, indeed, fairly saturated with performances and recordings of the same few hundred songs. The repertoire for Beyond was researched by Yannis François, whose unearthing of numerous manuscripts resulted in nine world-premiere recordings. A few of the songs were more familiar, but for most of the audience, the performance would have been a wholly novel experience.

Even the orchestra is costumed to cohere, with the theme of black marble and gold striations permeating the aesthetic. Between Orlinski's theatrical contributions, the visually-stimulating décor and lighting, and the unfamiliar music, the audience is brought closer to experiencing a kind of Gesamtkunstwerk than ever before. And they were visibly moved, calling, ultimately, for three encores from Orlinski and Il Pomo d'Oro.

What does this say about our appetite for classical music? A generation earlier, such innovations would have been unthinkable. The concert and recital were sacrosanct in their reverence to music in its most unadulterated form.

Are we to accuse audiences today of simply having shorter attention spans, being more impatient for cheap thrills, and demanding more visual stimulation to hold their attention? Orchestras across North America give live performances of cinematic orchestral scores, while the film plays on the big screen overhead. Is this, too, a symptom of the downfall of classical music as an experience unto itself?

Before we accuse audiences, before we jump on the bandwagon of conservatism, let us not forget that the rarified and inviolable atmosphere of the concert hall is, itself, the novelty.

Audiences of the 19th century and earlier were rowdy, talkative, and largely inattentive. Music, for most of its career across civilization, played a complementary role in a given experience, whether serving to accompany a theatrical performance, as was the case from at least as early as Ancient Greece, to buoying up religious ceremonies with chants and hymns that included audience participation, or, more secondarily, simply as light background entertainment while people ate, drank, and talked.

The expectation that an audience sit in rapt attention with 'merely' something to listen to is, itself, anachronistic, a nostalgia for a past that never was.

Let us not speak of competing with phones, films, or video games for audience attention. This is to look at the matter the wrong way around. People have always been drawn more readily to that which is more stimulating. Rather, let us have more performers and institutions take a page from Orlinski's book, and explore all avenues of the experience of music, to tell a story again, and draw the audience together into a single, collective experience - for, indeed, that was always the point.

Author: SCOTT BROOKS

Scott has been working in the arts for the past twenty years, since his start in the opera performance program at the University of British Columbia.

After completing his undergraduate degree there, he went on to pursue a PhD in Renaissance English literature.

Since then, he has divided his time between singing, writing, and teaching. He currently resides in Vancouver.

未来的歌剧咏诵

——斯科特·布鲁克斯

最近,我听了男高音雅库布·约泽夫·奥林斯基与巴洛克专业管弦乐团 Il Pomo d'Oro 合作的独唱音乐会《超越》。演出曲目来自奥林斯基的同名专辑,也是与 Il Pomo d'Oro 合作录制,但做了些调整。

《超越》的曲目由雅尼斯·弗朗索瓦 (Yannis François) 研究和发掘大量手稿后,最终录制了九张世界首演的唱片,有些歌曲较为熟悉,但对于多数观众而言,这场演出是一次全新的体验。黑色大理石和金色条纹的美学主题贯穿整场演出,连管弦乐队也穿着与主题一致的服装。奥林斯基的精彩演绎、陌生的音乐、充满视觉冲击的舞台布置和灯光,使观众比以往任何时候都更接近体验一种整体歌剧艺术。他们明显被感动了,最终要求奥林斯基和 Il Pomo d'Oro 再出场三次。

来自古典音乐领域年轻、才华横溢、雄心勃勃的表演者们对前代沉闷的演出规范,发出不同的声音。当我们考虑歌剧和声乐独奏会的未来发展时,这场音乐会特别有启发性。奥林斯基倾力使现场体验在主题上连贯;并作为中心表演者,向观众展示他对音乐的清晰诠释。他有意加入一些惊人的,看似不合时宜的表演元素,例如一系列表征失恋者痛苦和悲伤的霹雳舞动作。他在舞台上的多数活动被视为背叛传统的歌剧礼仪。

这说明了我们对古典音乐的热爱吗?上一代人,这样的创新是不可想象的。音乐会和独奏会是神圣不可侵犯的,它们崇敬最纯粹的音乐。难道只是责怪当今观众注意力持续时间短,需要更多的视觉刺激来吸引他们的注意力吗?北美各地的管弦乐队现场演奏电影管弦乐,而电影则在头顶的大屏幕上播放。这是否也是古典音乐本身作为一种衰落的征兆?

在我们指责观众之前,在我们加入保守主义的潮流之前,让我们不要忘记,音乐厅稀缺的、不可侵犯的氛围本身就是新奇事物。

19世纪及更早的观众吵闹、健谈，而且大多心不在焉。音乐在整个文明中的大部分时间里，都在特定的体验中扮演着补充角色，无论是作为戏剧表演的伴奏（至少从古希腊开始），还是通过观众参与的圣歌和赞美诗，或者更次要的是，在人们吃饭、喝酒和聊天时，音乐只是一种轻松的背景娱乐。期望观众全神贯注地坐着，'仅仅'听听音乐，这本身就是不合时宜的，是对从未有过的过去的怀念。

不要谈论与手机、电影或视频游戏争夺观众的注意力。这是从错误的角度看待这个问题。人们总是更容易被更刺激的东西吸引。相反，让我们请更多的表演者和机构借鉴奥林斯基的做法，探索音乐体验的所有途径，重新讲述一个故事，并将观众吸引到一个单一的音樂体验中——事实上，这一直是重点。

作者：斯科特·布鲁克斯

斯科特·布鲁克斯与艺术有不解之缘。

他于不列颠哥伦比亚大学学习歌剧表演，在完成本科学位后，继续研究文艺复兴时期英国文学并获得博士学位。

在过去的二十年里，斯科特醉心于歌剧、写作和教学。目前他居住在温哥华。

Smile

-By James B. S.

Auspicious smiling of
Bhaisajyaguru
Radiant in all directions
Cooling the unseen fires
Fueled by endless
Lust and Ignorance

The Earth
Ark of humanity
Rests at ease in
Halo of the smile

When my eyes light on
The Medicine Buddha,
Time disappears, and
A smile blossoms
On my own face.

Bhaisajyaguru or Bhaishajyaguru, formally Bhaisajya-guru-vaidurya-prabha-raja ('Medicine Master and King of Lapis Lazuli Light' in Sanskrit) is the Buddha of the eastern Pure Land of 'Pure Lapis Lazuli'.

In the small area of
3 centimeters between the ears
2.7 centimeters, chin to hairline,
An artisan has delicately crafted
The auspicious signs of the Buddha:
Slender nose with a straight bridge,
Beneath crescent eyebrows,
Long, curved eyelids over
Half-closed eyes, deep and soft,
Jutting lips of equal fullness
Uplifting a serene smile,
Plump cheeks like a noble lion,
Long ears like lotus petals,
Ushnisha, towering with nine layers
Of tiny curls, swirling right, vividly,
The dot between eyebrows, urna,
A whorl of hair, like cotton-wool,
A full and soft neck -
Characteristics of Greatness
Brought to life
Under meticulous hands,
Visage of the Medicine Buddha,
Hinting at liberation from suffering
And profound peace
Surpassing all understanding!

Part of 32 signs:
Blue-toned eyes, deep as the sea, demonstrate the Buddha's pleasantness of mind and his ability to see all enmities.

His lion's cheeks are because of the vow, "Any may come and ask, and I shall give as they desire to have."

The Ushnisha is a protuberance at the top of the head, and symbolizes a mind devoid of harm, as well as the Buddha's ability to dispense healing.

Bodily hair all curls to the right, turning towards the sun and away from ignorance.

Urna, the circle of hair between the eyebrows shows the teaching of sentient beings who learn the path of enlightenment.

The plump neck is derived from sacrificing what one loves and giving to sentient beings.

The Mahapurusalaksana (Great Man's Marks in Sanskrit) are specific details about the Buddha's hands, feet, and overall physique, reflecting his spiritual purity and enlightened state.
The 32 Signs of a Great Man are described in the Pali canon, the most complete collection of early Buddist scriptures, as well as the Mahavastu, a hagiography of the Buddha.
The 80 Minor Characteristics of the Buddha are part of the Chinese Buddhist canon, and in the Pali canon are listed in the Apadana and the Milindapañha.
The deep blue of lapis lazuli is the distinctive color of the Medicine Buddha, symbolizing infinite healing and all-encompassing wisdom.

Left hand in Dhyana Mudra, a Amrita jar on it

The left hand faces upward, fingers extended, placed on the lap. This is the Dhyana Mudra, a meditation gesture symbolizing spiritual perfection, concentration of good law, and the overcoming of the world of appearance through enlightenment.

A three-leaf jar full of Amrita is in the left hand. 'Amrita' means immortality in Sanskrit, and was thought of as an elixir. It is synonymous with soma, the drink of the devas in the Vedic tradition. In Chinese Buddhism, Amrita is produced by a deep state of meditation, flowing from the pituitary gland into the back of the throat, and is the divine nectar that grants immortal life.

Right hand in Varada Mudra, holding a stem of myrobalan

The right palm facing outward, resting on the knee, with the fingers naturally curved toward the ground, is the Varada Mudra, a gesture of offering, giving, and compassion. The thumb and forefinger hold the stem of the myrobalan tree, the berries of which are said to cure all physical and mental illnesses. The myrobalan is sacred in the traditions of both Buddhism and Hinduism. The Amrita jar and myrobalan together are the symbols of the Medicine Buddha, sometimes depicted as a bowl and a single berry.

2500-years ago, as seen through the divine eye of Buddha, the cosmology of the universe was beyond imagination, even when compared with the findings of contemporary science. The cosmos, called Trisahassi Mahasassi Lokadhatu in Sanskrit or Trichiliocosm, consists of billions of Culanika Lokadhatu or 'thousandfold small world-systems', i.e., galaxies.

Thangka of constellation, painting on cotton, second half 18th century, private collection, photograph by NuoBu WangDian

The notion of the eastern world of lapis lazuli, the pure land, derives from the vows of the Medicine Buddha. It is located east of our Saha world, at a distance measured in the sand of ten Ganges rivers. In 'Sutra of the Medicine Buddha', when Bhaisajyaguru was treading the bodhisattva path, he solemnly made Twelve Great Vows. We present them here, using Minh Thanh and P.D. Leigh's translation (Sutra of the Medicine Buddha, 2001):

Thangka of Medicine Buddha Mandala, painting on cotton, second half 18th century, private collection, photograph by NuoBu WangDian

First Great Vow: In a future life, when I have attained perfect Enlightenment, brilliant rays will shine forth from my body, illuminating infinite realms. This body will be adorned with the Thirty-Two Marks of Greatness and Eighty Auspicious Characteristics. Furthermore, I will enable all sentient beings to become just like me.

Second Great Vow: In a future life, when I have attained perfect Enlightenment, my body, inside and out, will radiate far and wide the clarity and flawless purity of lapis lazuli. The light will awaken the minds of all beings dwelling in darkness, enabling them to engage in their pursuits according to their wishes.

Third Great Vow: In a future life, when I have attained perfect Enlightenment, I will, with infinite wisdom and skillful means, provide all sentient beings with an inexhaustible quantity of goods to meet their material needs.

Fourth Great Vow: In a future life, when I have attained perfect Enlightenment, I will set all who follow heretical ways upon the path to Enlightenment.

Fifth Great Vow: In a future life, when I have attained perfect Enlightenment, I will help countless sentient beings who cultivate the path of morality to observe the rules of conduct (Precepts) to perfection, in conformity with Three Root Precepts.

Sixth Great Vow: In a future life, when I have attained perfect Enlightenment, sentient beings who are disabled or suffering from illnesses in any form will, upon hearing my name, acquire well-formed bodies, endowed with intelligence, with all senses intact. They will be free of illness and suffering.

Seventh Great Vow: In a future life, when I have attained perfect Enlightenment, sentient beings with various illnesses, with no one to help them, nowhere to turn, will be relieved of their illnesses and enjoy home and family as soon as my name passes through their ears. Eventually they will realize unsurpassed enlightenment.

Eighth Great Vow: In a future life, when I have attained perfect enlightenment, the women who are undergoing sufferings and tortures, seeking for transformation into men, will, upon hearing my name, all be reborn as men. They will be endowed with noble features and eventually realize unsurpassed enlightenment.

Ninth Great Vow: In a future life, when I have attained perfect enlightenment, I will help all beings escape from the demons' net and free them from the bonds of heretical paths. Should they be caught in the thicket of wrong views, I will lead them to cultivate the practices of Bodhisattvas and realize unsurpassed enlightenment.

Tenth Great Vow: In a future life, when I have attained perfect enlightenment, those who are shackled, beaten, imprisoned, condemned to death or otherwise subjected to countless miseries and humiliations by royal decree, need only hear my name to be freed from all these afflictions, by the awesome power of my merits and virtues.

Eleventh Great Vow: In a future life, when I have attained perfect enlightenment, if those who suffer from starvation and committed a crime to obtain food should succeed in reciting my name single-mindedly, I will satisfy them with the most exquisite food and establish them in the realm of peace and happiness.

Twelfth Great Vow: In a future life, when I have attained perfect enlightenment, sentient beings who suffer from poverty, tormented by mosquitoes and wasps day and night, should recite my name single-mindedly. They will immediately receive all manner of exquisite clothing, adornments, music and entertainment to their heart's content.

Pure Land of Bhaishajyaguru, circa 1319. Dry fresco. Dimension in meters: 7.5 (H) x 15.1 (W), New York, Metropolitan Museum of Art (Accession Number: 65.29.2)

The mural, was once adorned the east wall of the main hall in the Lower Guangsheng (Vast Triumph) Temple, in the northern Chinese province of Shanxi. Bhaishajyaguru sits in a lotus position on the throne, surrounded by an assembly of deities. The Twelve Guardian Generals, standing at each side of the mural symbolize the twelve great vows of Medicine Buddha.

Seated Medicine Buddha, copper-alloy, gilt-lacquered, circa 1583. Dimension in centimeters: 19.8 (H) x 11.8 (W) x 8.2 (D), private collection, photographs by author

The Medicine Buddha sitting on the lotus pedestal is lithe and poised. Note the youthful vitality of the body and the slenderness of the limbs.

The shoulders are relaxed and broad, expressing strength and resilience. The limbs are delicately crafted and elongated, suggesting elegance and agility. The depiction altogether is a manifestation of the Buddha's inner strength.

The Buddha is sitting in lotus position, or Padmasana, the legs crossed, flat soles with swelled toes facing upward, placed on opposite thighs. The openness of the legs and soles reflects the Buddha's readiness to impart his teachings and compassion to all beings.

Lotus grows up from the mud, but emerges flowering, beautiful and pristine, above the water, serving as a potent metaphor, symbolizing purity, spiritual awakening, and the potential of all beings to rise above the murk of materialism and achieve enlightenment.

The tripod posture is considered the most stable one for meditation, signifying the Buddha's unwavering concentration and Samadhi (deep meditative state) that leads to his enlightenment. The symmetry of the lotus position represents the Middle Way, a central concept in Buddhism that advocates a balanced approach to all things, and avoidance of extremes.

Adorning the Buddha's figure is a mantle that drapes over one shoulder and flows softly over the body.

Typically the Buddha's mantle is depicted as quite simple, but this one integrates a unique and sophisticated design with exceptional craftsmanship. A lush pattern of interlaced flora and fauna permeates the entirety of the robe. This goes beyond simple luxury: each motif is a lesson in Buddhist teachings, intricately woven into the robe's fabric.

The mantle with exquisite patterns

Descending dragon, head facing amrita jar

Dragon on the left arm

Engraved upon the chest of the robe is a magnificent dragon, descending from the heavens. With its head raised high, mouth agape in a silent roar, and eyes gazing upward, the dragon embodies boldness and command.

Two other dragons are placed prominently across the left arm and back right side of the robe, flying upward and grasping flaming pearls in claws. Three dragons represent the three jewels of Buddhism or Triratna, the Buddha, Dharma, and Samgha.

The first jewel represents the Buddha, who attained enlightenment and taught others.
The second jewel represents the fundamental teachings of the Buddha acquired on his quest for liberation.
The third jewel is the monastic community that the Buddha established during his life.

Dragon on back right side

Panlong pillar group in Dacheng Hall of Qufu Confucius Temple, Shandong Province China

The Dragon Stone Pillars of Dacheng Hall, Temple of Confucius in QuFu, Shandong Province, China. Dimension in meters: 5.98 (H) x 0.81 (W). Originally carved by Huizhou artisans around the Ming Hongzhi reign,1500 CE, they were re-carved in the second year of Yongzheng reign, Qing, 1724 CE, after a fire destroyed most of the sculptures.

In Asian mythology, dragons are powerful and benevolent creatures, revered as guardians of sacred teachings. The association between dragons and the protection of Buddhist sutras can be found in various historical texts, artworks, and temple motifs across China.

In the Lotus Sutra (Saddharma Pundarika Sutra), one of the most important Mahayana Buddhist texts, a dragon princess offers a precious jewel, her most valuable possession, to the Buddha, in exchange for the Dharma. Here, a dragon is shown valuing and protecting the Buddha's teachings.

The Tibetan Buddhist canon is replete with references to mythical beings and protectors of the Dharma, known as Dharmapalas. Among them, the Naga is a divine, or semi-divine, race of half-human, half-serpent beings with dragon-like attributes that are expressive of their role in guarding the teachings against corruption and obstacles.

Details of dragon pillar in Dacheng Hall

On the back of the mantle to the right hand side, the dragon rises above the treasure-filled offering bowl, and two peacocks delicately dance on either side, wings wide and resplendent.

At back of the mantle, two dancing peacocks on the bottom

Interlaced vines and scrolls frame the space, creating a sense of abundance and fertility, implying the flourish of Dharma.

Peacock on the left bottom

Peacocks symbolize the transformation of negative energies. Their natural ability to eat poisonous plants and snakes without being harmed expresses the idea of metamorphosing negative experiences into sources of strength and beauty.

The presence of four dancing peacocks, two placed on the mantle-covered calves and two behind, indicates one of the central concepts in Buddhism and the first teaching given by the Buddha: The Four Noble Truths.

Peacock on the right bottom

Two dancing peacocks on the mantle covering the calves

Peacock on the left calf

Peacock on the right calf

First Noble Truth: existence is suffering (duhkha)	The first Truth states that all existence is characterized by sufferings, and does not bring ultimate satisfaction. In the Saha World, birth, aging, sickness and death are the categories of the first suffering; the second is the suffering of separation from what is desired; the third is the union of what is undesired; the fourth is failing to obtain what one desires.
Second Noble Truth: suffering originates in desire (samudaya)	The second Truth explains the cause of the sufferings: the thirst (trishna) for sensual pleasures, the desire for permanence, the craving for becoming and unbecoming and the clinging to self-centered views. They bind beings to the cycle of existence (samsara).
Third Noble Truth: suffering ends when desiring ends (nirodha)	The third Truth says that through elimination of craving, suffering can be brought to an end. This state of cessation is called Nirvana, where one is free from the cycles of birth, death, and rebirth (samsara).
Fourth Noble Truth: the way to end desire and suffering is the Eightfold Noble Path (marga)	The fourth Truth gives the Eightfold Noble Path as the means for the ending of suffering. This path is a practical guide to ethical and mental development with the goal of freeing the individual from attachments and delusions, ultimately leading to understanding, wisdom and Nirvana.

Qilin on the left thigh, head facing right up

Qilin on the right thigh, head facing left up

An image of a qilin as depicted in the work Sancai Tuhui (三才圖會) from the Ming dynasty, circa 1609

Two half-kneeling qilins are wrapped around both thighs, heads facing the Medicine Buddha, eyes attentive and alert, portraying great respect.

The qilin, a legendary creature with the body of a deer, head of a dragon, hooves of a horse and tail of an ox, is renowned for its benevolent nature. Qilins move swiftly and meticulously to avoid harming those in their ecosystem out of compassion – one of the paramount values in Buddhism.

In various cultural contexts, the qilin is associated with the granting of good fortune and gifting of healthy offspring. It appears with the imminent arrival of a sage or illustrious ruler.

In the context of the youthful expression of Medicine Buddha and the first teaching, it is very likely that qilins, dragons and peacocks gather together to celebrate an extraordinary moment – the enlightening of Bhaisajyaguru.

The Primordial Buddha Vajradhara, circa 15th century, New York, Metropolitan Museum of Art (Accession Number: 41.160.97a, b), pedestal with double lotus pedal

Pedestals of buddha's figures seen in museums are often depicted in one or multiple layers of lotus pedals.

The pedestal of the seated Medicine Buddha is illustrated in relief carving, with a grand ritual ceremony comprised of fifteen vivid figures lined up in front, and a Dharmachakra with interlaced lotus patterns at the back. It is echoing the celebration of Buddha's enlightenment.

A grand ritual ceremony with fifteen figures lined up

The fifteen figures are divided into two groups. There are six guards of honor across the front: the first playing tingsha (cymbal), the second holding a tribute box, the third raising a Dhvaja, the fourth with four heads and four arms, holding a conch shell in the left upper hand, probably represents the Kalachakra (the wheel of time) and the fifth and sixth with long skirts, guiding the second group forward.

Six guards of honor across the front, as the first group

The Dhvaja (victory banner) is one of the eight emblems of Buddhism, standing for the Buddha's victory over the four Maras, or hindrances to enlightenment.

Mara was a god who tried to distract and tempt Siddhartha Gautama (the Buddha) as he sat under the Bodhi tree seeking enlightenment. First, Mara called up a horde of demons, but Siddhartha did not fear them. Then he sent his most beautiful daughters to seduce Siddhartha, but before Siddhartha's eyes they turned into ugly hags. Finally Mara admitted defeat.

In early Buddhist texts and commentaries, the four Maras are traditionally presented as:

Klesha-Mara represents the afflictive emotions and behaviors such as greed, hatred, and delusion. These are mental states that cloud judgment, lead to suffering, and bind individuals to the cycle of rebirth.
Kama-Mara represents the temptations of sensual pleasures and desires that can distract from spiritual practice.
Mrityu-Mara represents the fear of death that can paralyze and prevent one from pursuing spiritual goals. It's a reminder of the impermanence of life and the urgency to practice diligently.
Deva-putra-Mara represents pride, ego, and the delusion of self, which can lead to overestimating one's own importance and abilities, thereby hindering true spiritual progress.

Victory Banners, Tibetan Temple, Bodhgaya

The second group is composed of nine lamas, some of them holding ritual objects, standing on a longboard, probably representing the Dharma vessel, symbolizing that Buddhist teachings are a vessel that carries sentient beings to Nirvana. The tallest figure, in the middle, likely a holy lama, holds a cannon for the ritual assembly, accompanied by eight lamas standing separately before and after him.

Nine lamas of the second group

The first lama carries a long vajra trident, representing the elimination of the three poisons (triviṣa) or three unwholesome roots (akuśala-mūla). These are delusion or ignorance, greed or sensual attachment, and hatred or aversion, and lead to all negative states.

The fourth and sixth lamas hold the parasols, one of eight emblems, embodying the protection of Dharma. The rest of the lamas hold different ritual tools, possibly bells, drums, vajra, phurba, etc.

The tall hats worn by lamas of Gelug school in a ritual ceremony, monks in front of the Tsuklahang, Pälkhor Chöde, Gyantse, Tibet Autonomous Region, China

The tall hat worn by the holy lama is the iconic ceremony hat of Gelug, the newest of four schools in Tibetan Buddhism, founded by Je Tsong Khapa (1357-1419).

The scene on the pedestal is a precious record of the early Monlam Prayer Festival, also known as the Great Prayer Festival, which was established in 1409 by Tsong Khapa.

This week-long festival is the biggest religious event in Tibet. Chanting Medicine Buddha Sutras and undertaking pilgrimages are part of the event.

The long vajra trident in the right arm of Padmasambhava, Padmasambhava statue at Ghyoilisang peace, Nepal

A fair inference is that the seated Medicine Buddha was an important commission by a Gelug monastery to commemorate the festival.

The depiction of the Medicine Buddha's enlightenment evokes the memory of the first time the festival was held.

The Eight Emblems of Buddhism, also known as the Eight Auspicious Symbols (ashtamangala), are significant in various traditions of Buddhism. They represent different aspects of the teachings and are often depicted in art and iconography. Here are the Eight Auspicious Symbols and their meanings:

Sutra Cover with Eight Buddhist Treasures. Silk kesi tapestry. 18th century, China. New York, Metropolitan Museum of Art (Accession Number: 2012.559)

The Parasol (Chatra): Symbolizes protection from harmful forces and a shelter from suffering.

The Treasure Vase (Kalasha): Symbolizes inexhaustible wealth and prosperity, as well as the teachings of the Buddha.

The Lotus (Padma): Represents purity and enlightenment. The lotus grows in muddy water but remains unstained, symbolizing the primordial purity of body, speech, and mind.

The Victory Banner (Dhvaja): Signifies the victory of the Buddha's teachings over ignorance and the overcoming of all obstacles.

The Golden Fish (Matsya): Represents happiness, fertility, and abundance. They signify the ability to swim freely without fear in the ocean of suffering.

The Conch Shell (Shankha): Symbolizes the spread of the teachings of Buddha and the deep, melodious sound of the Dharma.

The Endless Knot (Shrivatsa): Represents the interconnectedness of all things and the endless cycle of life and death. It also symbolizes the union of wisdom and compassion.

The Wheel of Dharma (Dharmachakra): Represents the Buddha's teachings and the path to enlightenment. It is often depicted with eight spokes, symbolizing the Noble Eightfold Path.

Parasol, Mandi district, India

Golden Fish, Mandi district, India

Treasure Vase, Mandi district, India

Lotus, Mandi district, India

Conch Shell, Mandi district, India

Endless Knot, Mandi district, India

Victory Banner, Mandi district, India

Wheel of Dharma, Mandi district, India

Seated Medicine Buddha with throne and torana, circa 1583. Dimension in centimeters: 41 (H) x 22.5 (W) x 12.5 (D), private collection

An elaborate throne and torana (throne back) with sophisticated figures and patterns, cast separately for the seated Medicine Buddha, enhances the solemn ambience, indicating the statue was an important commission.

The throne appears broad and lofty from the front because of the trapezoidal shape, which creates a forced perspective. In the front, two snow lions guard the Dharmachakra (Wheel of Dharma).

The eight spokes of Dharmachakra embody the Eightfold Noble Path (Aryastaigamarga), a core part of the Buddha's teachings.

Two snow lions and Dharma Wheel in front of throne, Dimension in centimeters: 9.2 (H), 12.5 (D), front bottom 22.5 (W), front up 18 (W), back bottom 17 (W), back up 12.5 (W)

Right side view of the throne

Top view of the throne

Right Understanding (Samma-ditthi) is a deep understanding of the Four Noble Truths. They elucidate the nature of suffering, its origin and the path leading to its cessation. Samma-ditthi encourages a perception of reality that is free from illusions and misconceptions.

Right Intention (Samma-sankappa), is the cultivation of benevolent and wholesome intentions that replace greed, hatred and delusion. It emphasizes the importance of compassion, loving kindness, renunciation and the fostering of an attitude of goodwill toward oneself and others, steering the mind away from harmful thoughts and emotions.

Right Speech (Samma-vaca) means abstaining from false speech, malicious speech, harsh words and idle chatter. Samma-vaca promotes truthfulness, harmony and efficiency in communication. It encourages speaking in ways that are trustworthy, meaningful and beneficial.

Right Action (Samma-kammanta) entails engaging in ethical conduct by avoiding actions that cause harm, such as killing, stealing and sexual misconduct. It fosters moral integrity and helps practitioners act with kindness and responsibility towards all living beings.

Right Livelihood (Samma-ajiva) emphasizes the importance of earning a living through ethical means that do not cause harm or exploitation. It involves choosing professions that contribute positively to society and avoiding occupations that harm others.

Right Effort (Samma-vayama) is the commitment to cultivating beneficial qualities and abandoning harmful ones. It involves four aspects: preventing the arising of unwholesome states, abandoning already arisen unwholesome states, cultivating wholesome states that have not yet arisen and maintaining and perfecting wholesome states already arisen.

Right Mindfulness (Samma-sati) is the practice of maintaining a clear and attentive awareness of reality. It involves mindfulness of the body, feelings, mind and phenomena, helping the practitioner remain present and aware, thus preventing heedless actions and thoughts.

Right Concentration (Samma-samadhi) refers to the development of mental focus. This involves practicing various forms of meditation, leading to states of deep tranquility and insight.

A dragon on left side of the throne

There is a dragon soaring in the clouds on each side and back of the throne. On the top and bottom of the throne, two layers of edges protrude in a stepped shape, carved with an intertwined floral pattern.

A dragon on back of the throne

The pillar of the torana and slot of throne

Back view of seated Medicine Buddha with throne and torana

The torana of seated Medicine Buddha is composed of two parts. On both sides of the lower half, there are pillars, inserted into the slots of the throne for structural stability. A crossbeam connects the two pillars, with a flaming halo in the middle, facing the head of the Medicine Buddha.

The upper half is a peaked arch ornamented by intricate figures. A garuda stands powerfully at the peak, with body and wings diving forward. It is a golden-winged bird, half human and half eagle, one of the eight legions of devas and nagas (Astasena).

They are Asuras, celestial beings and the protectors of Dharma. Being the predator of the naga, the garuda is sometimes depicted with a serpent in its claws. According to Buddhist mythology, the garudas and nagas were reconciled by the Buddha.

Two nagas under the garuda

A garuda on the top of torana

Beneath, two nagas meet each other, upper bodies tilting backward majestically, arms in dancing posture, like a blooming flower. They are associated with bodies of water, such as rivers, lakes and oceans, and have played an important role in the preservation and transmission of Buddhist Sutras.

Makara and lotus flower above right side of the crossbeam

Above each side of the crossbeam, a makara stands upside down, holding a giant lotus flower. These are mythical sea creatures, combining features of crocodile, elephant and fish.

This composite nature suggests overcoming duality and the journey from ignorance to enlightenment. Makaras, like nagas, are protectors of treasures and sacred spaces.

Side pillars, crossbeam, flaming halo of the torana

Top to bottom of each side pillar, there are young deva riding sharabhas, giant lotus flowers and flying apsaras.

An apsara and lotus flower

A young deva and sarabha

The sharabha is a powerful beast with a goat's head, lion's mane and horse's body and legs. Young deva and sharabha embody the protection of the Buddha's teaching and perfection of effort.

Apsaras are celestial beings known for their beauty, grace, and enchanting dance and music.

These heavenly nymphs are often depicted as flying and participating in the divine celebrations. Here apsaras echo the celebration of Medicine Buddha's enlightenment.

Crowned Buddha, Bronze, Pala period, India (Bihar), 10th-11th century, Dimension in centimeters: 32.1 (H) x 18.1 (W) x 13.3 (D), New York, Metropolitan Museum of Art (Accession Number:1993.311a, b.)

The earlier forms of torana in Tibet, before the 12th century, were influenced by India and Nepalese artistic tradition, featuring simple motifs. Some 12th-century toranas are ornamented with an elephant, a sharabha and a makara on either side, bottom up. There are a number of variations: sometimes the makara is replaced by goose, and other times a garuda is placed on the top.

Starting from the 13th to 15th century, motifs on toranas became more elaborate and distinctly Tibetan. From the 16th century onward, designs reached a high level of complexity and refinement. A 'six ornament' pattern became popular, bottom to top on each side including elephants, lions, young devas mounting sharabhas, makaras, nagas and garudas.

The celebration of Buddha's enlightenment, the exquisite mantle, elaborate torana and depictions on the pedestal, indicate the statue was a commemoration of the first Monlam Festival held in one of the Gelug school monasteries.

Narrow edge of the pedestal inserted into the hole of throne

Protruding garudas and nagas balance the torana

Split casting makes it possible to produce intricate and exquisite patterns for the torana and throne while allowing the seated Medicine Buddha to be cast alone. It is a thoughtful design for practitioners who can bring the sacred figure with them for meditation when traveling.

Meticulous craftsmanship is required to match three split casting parts perfectly. The bottom of the pedestal is extended by a narrow edge, inserted in the oval hole on the throne precisely.

A Halo on the torana is wreathed just behind Buddha's head. The protruding garuda and nagas not only creates dynamic rhythm, they also subtly move the center gravity of the torana forward, resting it against the Buddha's shoulder, allowing the torana to stand steadily.

The method used in making this statue is lost-wax casting, an ancient technique with a history spanning thousands years.

The process begins with the creation of a model of the statue in beeswax, which is then covered in a clay mold. Once the mold is heated, the wax melts away, leaving a cavity into which molten metal is poured.

After cooling, the mold is broken to reveal the metal statue, which is then finished and polished.

Melted bronze poured into the wax chamber at the Xolotl workshop in Tlalnepantla, State of Mexico

Lost-wax casting allows for intricate and highly detailed designs. It involves multiple steps, each of which requires time-consuming attention to detail.

Small mistakes at any stage can result in defects, even damage to the final work. Only highly skillful artisans are able to complete the casting successfully.

Clay mold of a European bronze statue, molten bronze from open top through various tubes into the mold

After casting, the statue undergoes 'chasing' to refine its details and textures.

This process uses small metal tools to enhance facial expressions, clothing patterns, and other intricate details that may have been lost or softened during casting.

The surface and interior of the statue is covered with black lacquer, which is made by soaking the statue in the sap of a lacquer tree, dissolving soot or charcoal to create a black pigment. After that, the lacquer is left to dry and harden. This process is repeated multiple times to form a durable and thick finish, protecting the underlying material from moisture and wear.

Thick black lacquer covers the inside of the throne

A shining gilding once covered the whole statue, vanished mostly through the flow of time. Gold leaf, only a few micrometers in thickness, was applied to the statue. The application is a delicate and meticulous process.

First gold was hammered into thin sheets and cut into small squares or rectangles. Then the artisan applied a layer of natural adhesive, traditionally made from collagen found in animal hides, bones and connective tissues, onto the surface of the statue.
With a brush or gilding knife, gold leaf was gently placed onto the surface smoothly and evenly. After the adhesive dried completely, the gilded surface was burnished to enhance its shine.

The remaining gilding on the statue

The artistic style of the seated Medicine Buddha, blending the features of the Central Plains of China, is attributed to the East Tibet area. Softer facial features, lighter body proportions, intertwined lotus patterns, qilin and dragon ornaments, are all evidence of this style.

The shapes of qilins, dragons and lotus flower conform to the style of the Ming Dynasty.

Bowl with Dragons, porcelain, Ming dynasty Zhengde mark and period (1506-21), Dimension in centimeters: 10.2 (H) x 15.6 (D), New York, Metropolitan Museum of Art (Accession Number: 25.216.3)

Dragon on left side of throne

Interlaced vine on the mantle

Lotus flower on the torana

Unknown author, Tsongkapa, thangka from Tibet in the 15th century, New York, Rubin Museum of Art

Je Tsongkhapa, the founder of Gelug school, was born in the Tsongkha area of Amdo, the region in historical eastern Tibet, now Huang Zhong County, Xining, Qinghai Province in China. In 1560 the meditator Tsöndrü Gyeltsen built a small monastery at the village of Lusar near Tsongkhapa's birthplace.

In 1576, the 3rd Dalai Lama, Sönam Gyatso, on his way to meet Altan Khan, bestowed as ' Shun Yi Wang' by Ming emperor, requested thatTsöndrü Gyeltsen construct a larger monastery and appointed him as the head Lama. In 1583 spring, the 3rd Dalai Lama presided over the Monlam Prayer Festival after monastery expansion was completed and gave it the name Ta'er temple or Kumbum Jampa Ling. Kumbum means "100,000 enlightening bodies of the Buddha".

The seated Medicine Buddha was very likely commissioned by the monastery at that time to commemorate the first Monlam Prayer Festival upon Ta'er temple's completion. The central figure may be the 3rd Dalai Lama, Sönam Gyatso.

That time monasteries played a central role in Tibet society and often had workshops or resident artists around it. Making of buddhism statues was considered a highly meritorious act, and thus, the identities of individual artists were often not recorded, as the focus was on the religious significance of the work rather than personal acclaim. This practice is mirrored in Western Christianity.

Statue of Tsongkhapa, founder of Gelugpa Sect (Yellow Hats) in Ta'er temple near Xining, Qinghai, China.

Handle and display buddhism statues properly:

Place Buddha Statue appropriately, photograph by author

Always handle Buddha statues with respect. Before moving or touching the statue, it can be beneficial to take a moment of silence, offering respect or a short prayer, if you are inclined. When lifting or carrying a Buddha statue, use both hands and hold it respectfully at chest level or higher. Avoid holding the statue by its head or extremities.

Ideally, the statue should face east, the direction of the rising sun, symbolizing enlightenment. If this is not practical, then it should face into the room or space in a welcoming manner. Be sure to place it in a respectful location, on a shelf or altar in a quiet space. It should not be placed on the floor, in bedrooms or near bathrooms.

References:

Robert E. Buswell Jr., Donald S. Lopez Jr. (2013). 'The Princeton Dictionary of Buddhism'. Princeton University Press, ISBN 978-1-4008-4805-8.

Damien Keown (2004). 'A Dictionary of Buddhism'. Oxford University Press, ISBN 978-0-19-157917-2.

David Webster (2005). 'The Philosophy of Desire in the Buddhist Pali Canon'. Routledge. ISBN 978-0-415-34652-8.

Steven M. Emmanuel (2015). 'A Companion to Buddhist Philosophy'. John Wiley & Sons, ISBN 978-1-119-14466-3.

Carl Olson (2009). 'The A to Z of Buddhism'. ISBN 978-0-8108-7161-8

TW Rhys Davids, William Stede (1993), 'Pali-English Dictionary', Motilal Banarsidass Publ., ISBN 8120811445

Ingrid Fischer-Schreiber (University of Vienna), Franz-Karl Ehrhard (University of Hamburg), Michael S. Diener (Japanologist, Tokyo). Translated by Micheal H. Kohn (1991) , 'A Concise Dictionary of Buddhism and Zen'. ISBN 978-1-59030-808-0

Guang Xing (2004). 'The Concept of the Buddha: Its Evolution from Early Buddhism to the Trikaya Theory'

Image Sources:

Pure Land of Bhaishajyaguru, New York, Metropolitan Museum of Art (Accession Number: 65.29.2, metmuseum.org/art/collection/search/42716)

Sān, Lie, Panlong pillar group in Dacheng Hall of Qufu Confucius Temple, commons.wikipedia.org/wiki/File:曲阜孔庙大成殿盘龙柱群.jpg

Sancai Tuhui qilin (三才圖會) from the Ming dynasty, circa 1609, commons.wikimedia.org/wiki/File:Qilin_in_sancai_tuhui.jpg

The Primordial Buddha Vajradhara, circa 15th century, New York, Metropolitan Museum of Art (Accession Number:41.160.97a,b, metmuseum.org/art/collection/search/39141)

Victory Banners, Tibetan Temple, Bodhgaya, commons.wikimedia.org/wiki/File:070_Victory_Banners_(9227905154).jpg

Vajra trident in the right arm of Padmasambhava, Christopher J. Fynn, Padmasambhava statue at Ghyoilisang peace, Nepal, commons.wikimedia.org/wiki/File:Guru_-_Boudha.jpg

Monks in front of the Tsuklahang, Pälkhor Chöde, Gyantse, Tibet Autonomous Region, China, commons.wikimedia.org/wiki/File:TIB-gyantse-tsuklakhang-mönche.jpg

Sutra Cover with Eight Buddhist Treasures, Silk kesi tapestry, 18th century, China, New York, Metropolitan Museum of Art (Accession Number: 2012.559, metmuseum.org/art/collection/search/78284)

John Hill, Eight Auspicious Symbols, India, commons.wikimedia.org/wiki/File:Four_auspicious_symbols,_Mandi,_HP.jpg

Crowned Buddha, bronze, Pala period, India (Bihar), 10th-11th century, New York, Metropolitan Museum of Art (Accession Number:1993.311a.b, metmuseum.org /art/collection/search/39189)

Clay mold of a European bronze statue, molten bronze from open top through various tubes into the mold, commons.wikimedia.org/wiki/File:Fosa_en_bronze_inacabada_Museu_de_Belles_Arts_de_Copenhaguen.jpg

Thelmadatter, Melted bronze poured into the wax chamber at the Xolotl workshop in Tlalnepantla, State of Mexico, commons.wikimedia.org/wiki/File:Xolotl028.jpg

Bowl with Dragons, New York, Metropolitan Museum of Art (Accession Number:25.216.3 metmuseum.org/art/collection/search/42525)

Unknown author, Tsongkapa, thangka from Tibet, New York, Rubin Museum of Art, commons.wikimedia.org/wiki/File:Tsongkapa,_thangka_from_Tibet_Google_Art_Project.jpg

Mario Biondi, Statue of Tsongkhapa, Ta'er Temple Qinghai, China, commons.wikimedia.org/wiki/File:Tsongkhapa.Kumbum.jpg

Sealed bottom of Buddhist deity Vajradhara, New York, Metropolitan Museum of Art (Accession Number:1975.1.1442, metmuseum.org/art/collection/search/460573)

Buddha's Tooth, commons.wikimedia.org/wiki/File:Buddha_Tooth.jpg

A bone relic of the Buddha, Famen Temple, China, commons.wikimedia.org/wiki/File:Famen_Si_May_2007_052.jpg

微笑

药师佛
祥和微笑
遍照虚空
平息
无明和慾望
之焰

地球
人类方舟
释然於
微笑中

当我凝视
药师佛
时间幻灭

微笑
在我脸上
绽放

药师佛又名药师琉璃光王佛或消灾延寿药师佛，其名源于梵文"Bhaiṣajya-guru-vaiḍūrya-prabhā-rāja"，音译"鞞杀社 窶噜 薛琉璃 钵喇婆 喝啰阇也"。药师佛的国土称"东方琉璃世界"或"东方琉璃净土"。

两耳之间3厘米
下额至髮际2.7厘米
方寸之中
巧匠能工
吉祥佛颜：

鼻梁俊秀
月眉下弯
双眸半闭
柔和深邃
嘴唇丰满
笑容安详
狮颊高贵
长耳垂肩
顶有肉髻
高耸九层
发螺右旋
眉间白毫
细泽绵长
颈项丰腴

妙手细琢
药师圣貌
静寂清澄
超越一切！

部分三十二相好：

佛眼深邃如海源于佛陀的慈悲心和洞察一切。

佛陀脸颊犹如狮子源于佛陀的誓言："任何人都可以来求，我将给予他们想要的东西。"

头顶肉髻源于佛陀的心念远离一切伤害，以及治愈众生烦恼的能力。

身毛右卷源于远离无明。

眉间白毫源于教导众生学习证悟之道。

丰腴颈项源于牺牲所爱布施众生。

三十二相和八十随好，又称大丈夫相，源于梵文，描述转轮圣王和佛陀的体貌特征。在《中阿含经》、《长阿含经》、《大般若经》等巴利文藏经和大乘经典中有具体描述。

琉璃深蓝，代表药师佛消除一切疾病和空性智慧。

左手结禅定印,手掌托甘露宝罐,作者摄影

药师佛,左手结禅定印,手心朝上,手指展于腿前。是禅定冥想时所结手印,也称定印。象征着精神的完美、专注善法以及通过开悟超越轮回。

左手托着装满甘露的三叶宝罐。"甘露"在梵文中的意思是不朽,被认为是长生不老药。它是苏摩(soma)的同义词,苏摩是吠陀传统中天神的饮料。在汉传佛教中,甘露于深度冥想状态下产生,由脑下垂体流入喉部,是赋予不朽生命的圣露。

右手结予愿印,拇指和食指捏诃子枝,作者摄影

右手结予愿印,又称施予印、施愿印,右掌朝外,手指自然弯曲向地面。代表佛陀的给予和慈悲能满众生所愿。

拇指和食指握诃子树茎,据说其浆果可以治愈所有身心疾病。诃子在佛教和印度教的传统中都是圣物。甘露宝罐和诃子是药师佛的象征,有时被描绘成一个托钵碗和一粒诃子果。

2500年前,通过佛陀天眼所见的浩瀚宇宙,即使以现代科学的发现而言,亦超乎想象。佛陀所见宇宙由无数个'大千世界'组成,在梵语中被称为 'Trisahassi Mahasassi Lokadhātu 或 Trichiliocosm'。每个'大千世界'由数十亿个小世界组成,其中一千个小世界,名一小千世界,一千个小千世界名一中千世界,一千中千世界名一大千世界。

星象运行图,唐卡,棉布,十八世纪下半叶,私人收藏,诺布·旺典摄影

东方琉璃世界由药师佛的大愿而成,位于人类所居娑婆世界的东边,距离十恒河沙之遥(恒河是南亚主要河流,流经印度和孟加拉国,全长2525公里)。

《药师佛经》中,药师佛成佛前行菩萨道时,曾庄严发十二大愿:

药师佛坛城,唐卡,棉布,十八世纪下半叶,私人收藏,诺布·旺典摄影

第一大愿：愿我来世得阿耨多罗三藐三菩提时，自身光明炽然，照耀无量无数无边世界，以三十二大丈夫相、八十随形，庄严其身；令一切有情，如我无异。

第三大愿：愿我来世得阿耨多罗三藐三菩提时，以无量无边智慧方便，令诸有情，皆得无尽所受用物，莫令众生有所乏少。

药师佛净土，壁画，约1319年，规格（米）：7.5（高）x 15.1（宽），纽约，大都会艺术博物馆（藏品号：65.29.2，metmuseum.org/art/collection/search/42716）。这幅壁画曾位于中国山西省北部广胜寺下院正殿东壁。药师佛结跏趺坐于宝座上，周围环绕着众菩萨和神将。壁画两侧的十二神将象征着药师佛的十二大愿。

第二大愿：愿我来世得阿耨多罗三藐三菩提时，身如琉璃，内外明彻，净无瑕秽，光明广大，功德巍巍，身善安住，焰网庄严过于日月；幽冥众生，悉蒙开晓，随意所趣，作诸事业。

第四大愿：愿我来世得阿耨多罗三藐三菩提时，若诸有情，行邪道者，悉令安住菩提道中；若行声闻、独觉乘者，皆以大乘而安立之。

第五大愿：愿我来世得阿耨多罗三藐三菩提时，若有无量无边有情，于我法中修行梵行，一切皆令得不缺戒，具三聚戒。设有毁犯，闻我名已，还得清净，不堕恶趣。

第六大愿：愿我来世得阿耨多罗三藐三菩提时，若诸有情，其身下劣，诸根不具，丑陋顽愚，盲聋喑哑，挛躄背偻，白癞癫狂，种种病苦。闻我名已，一切皆得端正黠慧，诸根完具，无诸疾苦。

第七大愿：愿我来世得阿耨多罗三藐三菩提时，若诸有情，众病逼切，无救无归，无医无药，无亲无家，贫穷多苦。我之名号一经其耳，众病悉除，身心安乐，家属、资具悉皆丰足，乃至证得无上菩提。

第八大愿：愿我来世得阿耨多罗三藐三菩提时，若有女人，为女百恶之所逼恼，极生厌离，愿舍女身。闻我名已，一切皆得转女成男，具丈夫相，乃至证得无上菩提。

第九大愿：愿我来世得阿耨多罗三藐三菩提时，令诸有情，出魔罥网，解脱一切外道缠缚。若堕种种恶见稠林，皆当引摄置于正见，渐令修习诸菩萨行，速证无上正等菩提。

第十大愿：愿我来世得阿耨多罗三藐三菩提时，若诸有情，王法所录，绳缚鞭挞，系闭牢狱，或当刑戮，及余无量灾难凌辱，悲愁煎逼，身心受苦。若闻我名，以我福德威神力故，皆得解脱一切忧苦。

第十一大愿：愿我来世得阿耨多罗三藐三菩提时，若诸有情，饥渴所恼，为求食故，造诸恶业。得闻我名，专念受持，我当先以上妙饮食饱足其身，后以法味毕竟安乐而建立之。

第十二大愿：愿我来世得阿耨多罗三藐三菩提时，若诸有情，贫无衣服，蚊虻寒热，昼夜逼恼。若闻我名，专念受持，如其所好，即得种种上妙衣服，亦得一切宝庄严具、华鬘、涂香、鼓乐、众伎，随心所玩，皆令满足。

药师佛座像,铜合金,上漆和贴金工艺,约1583年,规格(厘米):19.8(高)、11.8(长)×8.2(宽),私人收藏,作者摄影

药师佛端坐于莲花座上，姿态轻盈，泰然自若。四肢修长，凸显青春体态和活力。肩膀宽阔而放松，表现出力量和韧性。四肢做工精致，体现优雅和强健，彰显药师佛内在力量。

跏趺坐姿，双腿交叉，大腿向两侧展开，脚心朝上，置于另一侧大腿之上。开放的腿部和脚心象征药师佛准备将他的教义和慈悲传授给一切众生。

莲花生于淤泥中，但出于水面而绽放，谓'出淤泥而不染'，象征着纯洁，隐喻精神升华及众生超越物质主义的暗蒙而觉醒的潜力。

锥形坐姿是最稳定的禅定姿势，象征着佛陀坚定不移的专注和成就开悟的三摩地（最深度的禅定状态）。对称的跏趺坐姿也代表了中道，佛教的核心教义之一，指平衡对待一切事物，避免极端。

图案繁复精美的袈裟，作者摄影

一件袈裟，披在药师佛肩上，轻覆全身。佛陀的袈裟通常简朴不加装饰，但此件袈裟，与众不同。

缠枝纹和动物纹饰，繁茂交错，遍布整件袈裟，错综复杂地编织，超越奢华，融合独到设计和卓越工艺。其中每件纹饰都深蕴佛教寓意。

前胸袈裟,龙从天而降,龙首对着宝瓶,作者拍摄

胸前袈裟刻着一条雄伟的巨龙,从天而降。龙头高高扬起,发出龙吟,眼睛向上凝视,象征着勇气和征服。

另有两龙位于左臂袈裟和背部右侧,向上飞翔,爪握火焰珠。三龙代表佛教三宝,即佛、法、僧。

龙位于左臂袈裟,作者拍摄

佛宝代表佛陀,他证悟并教导他人;法宝代表佛的一切教法,包括三藏十二部经典及八万四千法门;僧宝代表依诸佛教法如实修行、弘传佛法、度化众生的出家众。

龙位于后背袈裟右侧,作者拍摄

亚洲文化中，龙强大而仁慈，被尊为圣守护者。龙保护佛经的内容在中国各地的历史文献、艺术品和寺院装饰中都可找到。最重要的大乘佛教经典之一《法华经》中，龙王之女向佛陀献上一件她最珍贵的珠宝，以换取佛法。

藏传佛教经典中也大量提及佛法保护者（称为护法神）。其中，那伽族或蛇族是一个神圣的种族。他们是半人半蛇的神秘生物，有类似龙的属性，在他们保护下佛经免受侵害和失传。

中国山东省，曲阜孔庙大成殿盘龙柱，
commons.wikipedia.org/wiki/文件：曲阜孔庙大成殿盘龙柱群.jpg

背面袈裟，缠枝纹丰盛，隐喻佛法的繁荣。

底部两侧，孔雀展翅起舞，光彩夺目。孔雀食用有毒的植物和蛇而不受伤害，象征将负面的经历转化为力量和成长的源泉。

四只起舞孔雀，分列于后背底部两侧，及小腿处，作者拍摄

另有两只孔雀位于小腿袈裟上，四只起舞孔雀，象征佛陀首传之法-四圣谛：苦、集、灭、道。

苦谛以逼恼为义，生老病死；爱别离；冤憎会；求不得；人生实相是苦。

集谛以招聚为义。是所有苦的成因。

灭谛以灭无为义。灭谛是指灭除烦恼和生死之累，即为涅盘。

道谛以能通为义。正道及助道，二相扶，能通至涅槃。

大腿外侧袈裟上，两只麒麟，面朝药师佛，目光炯炯有神，以无上尊敬，半跪恭迎药师佛。

二只麒麟位于左右大腿外侧，跪迎药师佛，作者拍摄

麒麟，中国传说中的神兽，具有鹿身、龙头、马蹄、牛尾，以仁慈而闻名。

二只麒麟位于左右大腿外侧，跪迎药师佛，作者拍摄

它行动迅速而细致，以避免伤害其他动物，麒麟的同情心是佛教最尊崇的价值观之一。

麒麟的出现，预示圣人或英明统治者的面世，也与赐予好运和健康的后代联系在一起。

结合药师佛像青年活力的造型和四孔雀象征首传四谛法门，麒麟、龙、孔雀齐聚一堂，是共同庆祝一个非凡的时刻——药师佛开悟成道。

金刚总持,铜合金,鎏金,约15世纪,规格(厘米): 45.7(高) x 31.1(长) x 22.9(宽),纽约.大都会艺术博物馆(藏品号: 41.160.97a,b.)

博物馆所见佛像宝座多为一层或多层莲花宝座。

此药师佛坐像宝座,以浮雕呈现一场盛大法会,前部一字排列着十五个栩栩如生的人物,后部中央有一法轮,两侧为莲花缠枝纹。盛大法会与庆祝佛陀成道相呼应。

宝座前部,十五人一列,举行盛大法会;后部法轮

前六位组成法会仪仗队,作者摄影

十五个人物,分成两组。前面六位组成仪仗队,第一位敲钹,第二位捧着贡盒,第三位高举法幢,第四位四头四臂,左手握一法螺,可能代表"时轮金刚",第五和第六位着长裙,引导第二组前进。

法幢又称胜利旗幢，是佛教八吉祥之一，代表佛陀战胜阻碍开悟的四天魔。

天魔是掌管三十三天的天帝之一。当乔达摩·悉达多（佛陀俗家名）坐在菩提树下即将开悟成道时，他试图阻止。首先天魔召唤一群恶魔，但悉达多并不恐惧；随后他派出最美丽的女儿们去勾引悉达多，但她们在悉达多眼前变成了丑陋的女巫。最后天魔承认失败。

莲花缠枝纹，作者摄影

法幢，藏传寺庙，菩提伽耶

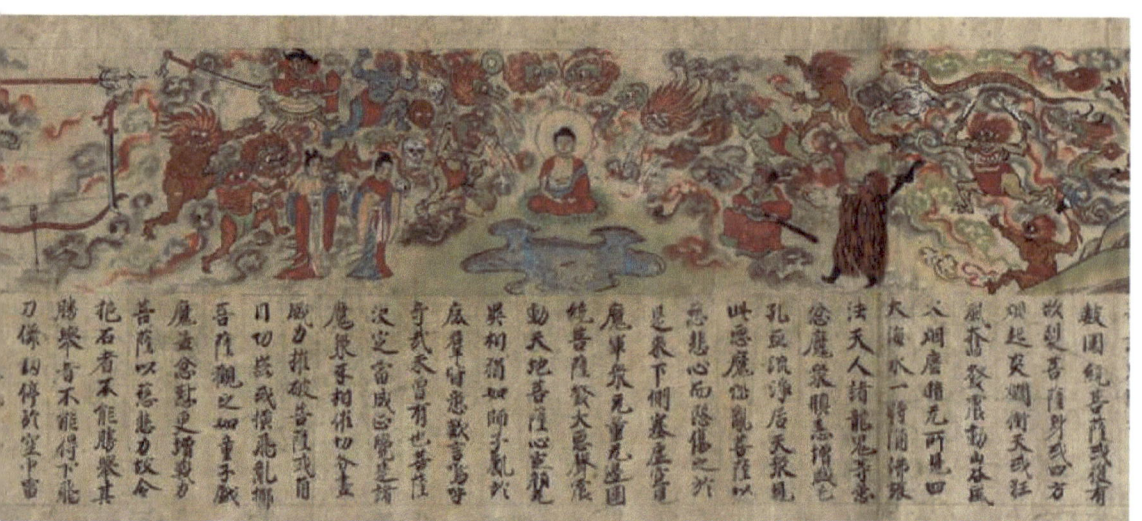

佛陀战胜天魔的场景,《过去现在绘因果经》,(松永本),日本,手卷;纸本设色,十三世纪末,纽约,大都会艺术博物馆(藏品号:2015.300.7)

在早期佛教经典和注释中,四天魔被描述为:

烦恼魔代表贪、嗔、痴等烦恼情绪和行为。这些心理状态会影响判断力,导致痛苦,并将个人束缚在轮回之中。

蕴魔代表感官享乐和欲望的诱惑,会分散精神修行的注意力。

死魔代表了对死亡的恐惧,这种恐惧会让人瘫痪。

天子魔代表骄傲、自我和妄想,这导致高估自己和自我设限,从而阻碍解脱。

第二组九位喇嘛,手持法器,立于一长板之上,长板象征渡众生入涅槃彼岸的法船。中间最高的一位代表地位崇高的主持喇嘛,手持经书主持法会,八位喇嘛分别站在他的前后。

第一位喇嘛手持金刚三叉戟,代表消除导致一切恶果的三毒或三不善根。这三者是痴、贪和嗔。

第四和第六位手持伞盖,亦为佛教八吉祥之一,象征对佛法的保护。其余喇嘛各持有不同的法器,可能为金刚铃、鼓、杵、钺等。

第二组九位喇嘛,作者摄影

主持喇嘛所戴高帽是格鲁派的标志性僧帽，格鲁派为藏传佛教四大宗派中最晚成立的一支，由宗喀巴大师（1357-1419年）创立。

基座上的场景是早期祈愿大法会的珍贵记录，又称默朗木大法会，由宗喀巴大师于1409年创立。为期一周的法会是西藏最大的宗教活动。诵读药师佛经和朝圣是活动之一。

袈裟描绘庆贺药师佛开悟成道，寓意全新开始或首次，以此推断，药师佛坐像应为格鲁派某寺院为纪念首次祈愿大法会而制作的重要佛像。

莲花：代表纯洁和开悟。莲花长于淤泥，而不染污，象征身、语、意根本清净。

法螺：象征着佛法的传播和法音的深沉悠扬。

盘长：代表万物的相互联系和生与死的无尽循环。它还象征着智慧与慈悲的结合。

佛教八宝经盖，缂丝覆毯，十八世纪中国，纽约，大都会艺术博物馆（藏品号：2012.559）

佛教八吉祥又称佛教八宝：

伞盖：象征着免受有害力量的保护和免受痛苦的庇护。

双鱼：代表幸福、生育和富饶，也象征无惧轮回之海，并自由地游出轮回。

宝瓶：象征取之不尽的财富和繁荣，及佛陀的教义。

法幢：象征着佛陀教义战胜无明和克服一切障碍。

法轮：代表佛陀的教义和觉悟之道。它通常绘有八根轮辐，象征着八正道。

药师佛座像、基座、背拱为分别铸造，带基座和背拱规格(厘米):41(高)×22.5(宽)×12.5(厚).作者摄影

药师佛坐像有分别铸造的基座和背拱，做工精美，气势庄严，凸显此尊造像不同凡响。

基座正面两只雪狮守护法轮，作者摄影

基座为梯形体，正面梯形底部宽22.5厘米，上部宽18厘米；背面梯形底部宽17厘米，上部宽12.5厘米。从前面或两侧观看，由于梯形的透视效果，基座显得高大宏伟。正面纹饰为两只雪狮守护中间的法轮。

基座为梯形体，作者摄影

雪狮，作者摄影

法轮有八根轮辐象征八圣道：

正见：正确的见解和观念，指如实了知世间和出世间因果的智慧，透过三法印，四圣谛，十二因缘等佛教教理观察宇宙万象而获得正知正见。

正命：以合法不损害他人的谋生方式来维持生命，乃至不贩卖众生、军火、杀生器具、醇酒、毒品或嫖赌等。若是出家众，则如法求衣服、饮食、坐卧具、医药等供身什物。

正思维：没有贪嗔等烦恼情况下，依正见观察、思维，如理地作出决定，故又称为正欲或正志。由正思维才能做出正确之身口意业的行为。

正勤：又称正精进，指精进努力离恶向善。正勤有四：未生善令生；已生善令住；未生恶令不生；已生恶令灭。

正语：即戒止口之四恶业，不妄语，欺骗；不两舌，搬弄是非；不恶口，骂人或刻薄、诽谤；不绮语，不花言巧语或说虚妄不实之言。

正念：既不生邪念，意念正道。以修行来说既是忆念正法，并保持它，称为正念；如无法保持，既是失去正念。

正业：正当的行为和举止，身、口、意三业清净。戒杀生、邪淫、偷盗等行为。

正定：禅定时正确用心：止（三摩地），即入定，心一境性，心念保持在单一之定境中；观（毗婆舍那），于定中生智慧，用佛法观察实相。

基座左侧,作者摄影

基座两侧及背面各雕一飞龙腾云,宝座上下两层边缘呈阶梯状凸出,雕有缠枝纹。

基座背面,作者摄影

光焰正对头部,作者摄影

药师佛坐像背拱由两部分组成,下半部两侧支柱插入基座的凹孔内固定,支柱间有横梁,横梁中间为一环形光焰,正对药师佛头部背面。

背拱下半部,作者摄影

上半部为尖拱形,饰以繁复纹案,在顶端立一尊大鹏金翅鸟,身躯向前俯冲,威风凛凛。大鹏金翅鸟呈半人半鸟形象,为天龙八部之一。

他们是佛法的保护者。大鹏金翅鸟捕食龙族,有时爪中会抓着一条蛇。根据经典记载,佛陀调解了大鹏金翅鸟和龙族的关系。

大鹏金翅鸟立于顶端,作者摄影

大鹏金翅鸟下方，两那伽相交，上身优雅后弯，双臂呈舞姿，犹如盛开花朵。那伽与河、湖和海相关，在保存佛经和佛法传播中发挥了重要作用。

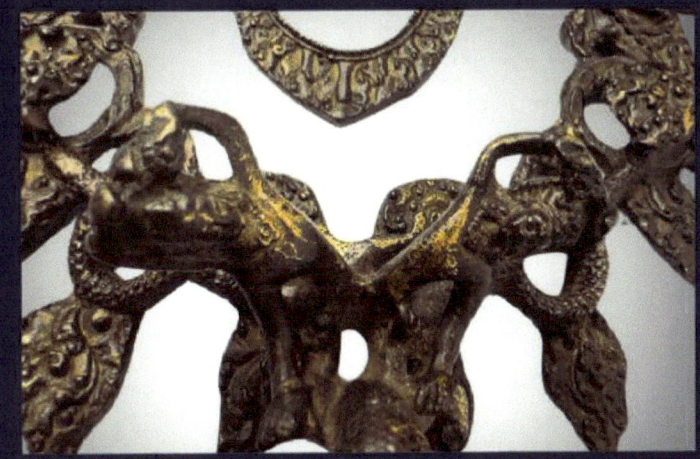

那伽相交呈舞姿，作者摄影

那伽于大鹏金翅鸟下方，作者摄影

横梁两侧上方，各有一只摩羯倒立，顶一朵巨型莲花。其为海中异兽，兼具鳄鱼、大象和鱼的特征。此复合形态暗示超越二元对立及从无明到开悟的历程。摩羯和那伽一样，是佛法的守护者。

摩羯倒立于横梁，作者摄影

右立柱,作者摄影

两边立柱由上至下,分别雕有骑着沙罗跋的小天神、大莲花和飞天。

沙罗跋和小天神,作者摄影

飞天,作者摄影

沙罗跋是一种威猛的神兽,形象为羊头、狮鬃和马身马腿。小天神和沙罗跋象征着护佑佛法和功德圆满。

飞天为天人,以美丽、优雅、动人舞蹈和音乐而闻名。这些天上的仙女经常以飞翔姿态展现于圣典。此处飞天正欢庆药师佛开悟成道。

西藏早期的背拱（公元12世纪之前）受印度和尼泊尔艺术影响，纹饰简单。一些公元12世纪的背拱装饰着大象、沙罗跋和摩羯，自下由上分列两侧。纹饰也有多种变化；有时摩羯被鹅代替，有时顶部放置金翅鸟。

从13世纪到15世纪，背拱纹饰演变为繁复精致，体现西藏特色。从16世纪开始，纹饰复杂和精致程度又更进一步，一种"六饰"纹样开始流行，由下自上，分别为大象、狮子、骑着沙罗跋的小天神、摩羯、那伽和大鹏金翅鸟。

佛陀成道的庆典、精美的袈裟、精致的背拱和宝座上的描绘，表明这尊雕像是为纪念格鲁派寺院举行的第一次祈愿法会而定制。

分体铸造使背拱和基座可以进一步精工细作，单独铸造的坐像则能从基座取下。对于修行者来说，是很实用的设计，方便外出时携带圣像修行。

此座造像以失蜡法铸造，这是一种拥有数千年历史的古老技术。首先用蜂蜡制作造像模型，然后用粘土模具覆盖。模具加热后，蜡融化，留下一个空腔，将熔融的金属倒入其中。冷却后，打破模具，露出金属造像，再进行精加工和抛光。

此造像表面和内部上黑漆，黑漆是漆树的树液混合烟灰或木炭而成。将造像浸没其中再取出晾干让漆干燥并变硬。这个过程重复多次，形成耐用而厚实的漆层，保护造像免受潮湿和磨损。

分体铸件需要精湛的工艺才能使各部分完美契合。经精心计算，药师佛座像底部一圈突起的窄边，精准地嵌入基座椭圆孔中，使座像严密固定在基座上。

失蜡铸造可以制作细节复杂丰富的造型。工艺复杂涉及多个工序，每个工序都需花费大量时间关注细节，任何小失误都会导致缺陷，甚至损坏最终作品，只有技艺高超的工匠才能成功完成铸造。铸造完成后，造像还需"雕琢"以完善其细节和纹理。在此过程中，会使用小型刻刀来增强各部位细节。

曾经整个造像覆盖着闪亮金箔，但随着时间的流逝，金箔大部已脱落。造像上贴的金箔厚度只有几微米。贴金过程非常精细，需要极大的耐心和精湛技艺。

横梁中间的光焰，也恰好位于佛陀头部的正后方。前凸的大鹏金翅鸟和那伽不仅动态优美，还巧妙地将背拱重心前移，靠在佛陀的肩膀上，使背拱平稳竖立。

佛像底部凸起窄边嵌入基座中稳稳将佛像固定在基座上，作者摄影

基座内部完整保留上漆工艺，作者摄影

首先，金子被锤成薄片，再切成小方块或长方形。然后艺人在雕像表面涂上一层天然粘合剂，这种粘合剂由动物皮、骨头和结缔组织中的胶原蛋白熬制而成。接着用小刷或贴金刀将金箔平滑均匀地轻捶在造像上。等粘合剂完全干燥后，对贴金表面进行抛光，以增强其光泽。

此尊药师佛座像的艺术风格融合了汉地特色，应铸造于藏东地区。其面部柔和，身体比例匀称，缠枝莲纹、麒麟纹、龙纹等特征均符合藏东地区造像特点。其麒麟纹、龙纹、缠枝莲纹的造型符合明代中晚期风格。

马铠甲颈甲和胸甲，皮革、铁、黄铜或铜合金，15-17世纪，中国西藏
规格（厘米）：左颈甲49.5（高）x 55.9（宽）；右颈甲50.2（高）x 55.9（宽）；胸甲48.3（高）x 62.2（宽），纽约，大都会艺术博物馆（藏品号：1997.242a-c，metmuseum.org/art/collection/search/26568）

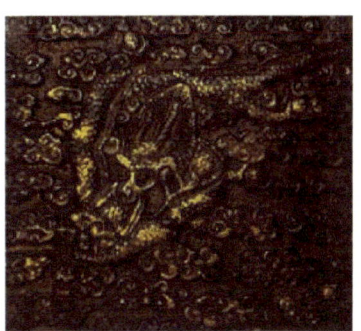

基座背面中央龙纹，作者摄影

明中期 缂丝龙纹圆补，规格（厘米）：38.1 x 38.1，纽约大都会艺术博物馆（藏品号：36.65.33，metmuseum.org/art/collection/search/65645）

此三件马铠甲，是目前已知西藏皮革马铠中保存最好、装饰最精美的。其装饰包括金色莲花、牡丹和其他花卉纹样，背景交替为红橙色、黑色和栗色；呈漆器效果，应该上有一层或多层着色漆；以金箔切出花卉纹样捶揲于皮革上、金箔之上再涂一层虫胶以保护金箔不脱落、虫胶上用细黑线绘制细节，并覆盖一层或多层桐油釉。此套马恺除装饰精美、做工精细，还非常坚固，可作防御盔甲，代表了西藏盔甲制作和皮革制品的最高水平。碳14测试，年代范围：1435-1665年

格鲁派创始人宗喀巴大师出生于安多宗喀地区，该地区位于历史上的西藏东部，即现在的中国青海省西宁市湟中县。

嘉靖三十九年1560年，禅修者仁钦宗哲坚赞在宗喀巴大师出生地附近的鲁萨村建造了一座小寺院。

万历四年1576年，第三世达赖喇嘛索南嘉措在前往会见蒙古俺答可汗途中第一次来到寺院并任命仁钦宗哲坚赞为该寺院住持，要求他扩建寺院。

第三世达赖喇嘛索南嘉措，伦敦威康收藏，commons.wikimedia.org/wiki/File:Sonam_Gyatso.jpg

第三世达赖喇嘛索南嘉措（1543-1588年）是第一个被尊为达赖喇嘛的人，此称号随后追溯授予他的两任前任。

明穆宗隆庆五年(1571年)，俺答可汗被封为中国顺义王，1578年，俺答可汗赐予索南嘉措"达赖喇嘛"的称号。"达赖喇嘛"源于蒙古语"达赖因汗"意为"大海之神"。

1900年的塔尔寺，照片由俄罗斯探险家 Gombojab Tsybikov 拍摄，commons.wikimedia.org/wiki/File:Цыбиков_Монастырь_Тумбум_Монголия_1900e.JPG

1583年初，第三世达赖喇嘛索南嘉措第二次到来为扩建寺院命名"塔尔寺"，赐赠供奉佛像和举办祈愿大法会。塔尔寺也称白塔强巴林，意为"十万佛菩萨"。

塔尔寺印经院, commons.wikimedia.org/wiki/File:A_Cover_of_Taer_Temple.JPG

药师佛座像极可能是寺院当时为纪念塔尔寺扩建落成后的第一届祈愿法会而特制，其中心人物很可能是第三世达赖喇嘛索南嘉措。

塔尔寺八塔，commons.wikimedia.org/wiki/File:Taersi.jpg

当时，寺院在西藏社会中扮演着重要角色，寺院内经常设有工坊或常驻艺术家。制作佛像被认为是一种功德无量的事业，因此艺术家的身份通常不会被记录下来，因为人们更看重作品的宗教意义，而不是个人的赞誉。

药师佛座像的底部已遗失，封在里面的圣物也已遗失。

座像内部中空，作者摄影　　　　座像底部遗失，作者摄影

在佛像内放置圣物是佛教中备受推崇的做法。这一传统被称为"装藏"，以赋予佛像之佛性内涵，使其成为神圣法器。

封于佛像内的圣物象征着佛陀的身、语、意；通常为价值连城的舍利、贵金属、宝石、珍贵药草、经书和圣咒等。

泰国至上尊者，僧王苏瓦哈诺（1913-2013）舍利，位于泰国孟程逸府班孔塔宝县，commons.wikimedia.org/wiki/File:Relics_of_buddha_from_His_Holiness_Supreme_Patriarch_of_Thailand_2012.jpg

公元前3世纪阿育王建造的佛塔，内有佛陀舍利，印度德里国家博物馆，commons.wikimedia.org/wiki/File:Buddhist_Stupa_containing_relics_of_Buddha,_National_Museum,_New_Delhi.jpg

日本的一座家庭佛龛，内有66位神道教和佛教神灵的塑像，英国威康收藏，commons.wikimedia.org/wiki/File:Domestic_shrine_Wellcome_L0043823.jpg

参考文献：

Robert E. Buswell Jr.; Donald S. Lopez Jr. (2013)。《普林斯顿佛教词典》。普林斯顿大学出版社，ISBN 978-1-4008-4805-8。

Damien Keown (2004)。《佛教词典》。牛津大学出版社，ISBN 978-0-19-157917-2。

David Webster (2005)。《佛教巴利文经典中的哲学》。劳特利奇出版，ISBN 978-0-415-34652-8。

Steven M. Emmanuel (2015)。《佛教哲学指南》。John Wiley & Sons，ISBN 978-1-119-14466-3。

Carl Olson (2009)，《佛教从 A 到 Z》，ISBN 978-0-8108-7161-8

TW Rhys Davids、William Stede (1993)，《巴利语-英语词典》，Motilal Banarsidass Publ.，ISBN 8120811445

Ingrid Fischer-Schreiber（维也纳大学）、Franz-Karl Ehrhard（汉堡大学）、Michael S. Diener（东京日本学家），由 Micheal H. Kohn 翻译 (1991)，《佛教与禅简明词典》，ISBN 978-1-59030-808-0

Guang Xing (2004)，《佛陀的概念：从早期佛教到三身理论的演变》

佛像安放礼仪：

始终以尊重的态度对待佛像。在移动或触摸佛像之前，应先清洁双手，触碰前安定心神片刻以表达敬意或默念佛像圣号。移动佛像时，请用双手端其底部，将佛像恭敬地举到胸前或更高位置。避免握住佛像的头部或四肢。

理想情况下，佛像应面向东方，即朝阳升起方位。如果不可行，那佛像应面向房间或空间入口。要安放在一个尊贵的位置，例如安静书房的高柜或供桌上，不应该放在靠近地板、卧室或浴室附近的位置。

Art Tour of Puerto Vallarta

-By James B.S.

Photographs by author

Arriving in Puerto Vallarta on a sunny day, I feel the breath of art and hot air at the same time. This beautiful coastal city on Mexico's Pacific coast, along with its nearby small towns, is a vibrant hub of creativity and culture. It is adorned with colorful murals, exotic handcrafted art, stylish buildings, and people with art in their blood.

Mexican muralism, graffiti and folk arts, full of fantasy and visual impact, have long inspired artists around the world. Here are a few notable examples:

Pablo Picasso (1881-1973)

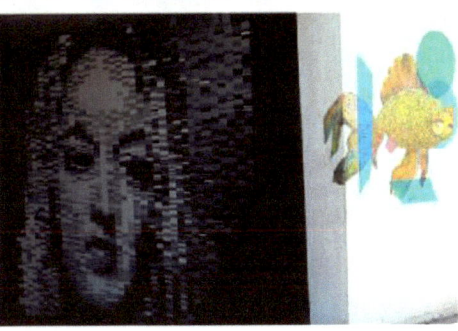

As a central figure in modern art, Picasso's works during and after the Spanish Civil War, particularly "Guernica," share thematic and stylistic connections with the murals of Mexican artists. His exploration of surrealism was enriched by his engagement with the works of Mexican contemporaries.

Picasso admired the way Mexican artists depicted social struggles and human suffering, themes that resonated deeply in his own work.

Diego Rivera (1886-1957)

Rivera is a quintessential Mexican painter whose large frescoes helped establish the mural movement in international art. His work is deeply rooted in Mexican culture and history, depicting the lives of indigenous people, the impact of colonization, and the struggles of the working class. Rivera's murals can be seen in public spaces around the world, bringing Mexican art to a global audience.

Salvador Dali (1904-1989)

The renowned Spanish surrealist artist, Dali, included Mexican influences in his striking and dreamlike work. For the 1939 New York World's Fair, Dali designed the "Dream of Venus" pavilion, which showcased a surreal environment blending various cultural influences, including elements reminiscent of Mexican art's bold and eclectic style. Dali's use of vibrant colors, fantastical imagery, and complex symbolism echoes the rich visual language of Mexican art.

Jean Charlot (1898-1979)

French-born artist Jean Charlot was deeply influenced by Mexican muralism and indigenous art. His collaboration with Rivera and his integration into the Mexican art scene allowed him to blend European techniques with Mexican themes, creating a unique fusion that resonated internationally.

Frida Kahlo (1907-1954)

Known for her many portraits, self-portraits, and works inspired by the nature and artifacts of Mexico, Frida Kahlo has inspired countless artists globally. Her use of vibrant colors and incorporation of Mexican folk art traditions have made her an iconic figure in both Mexican and feminist art movements.

Eduardo Chillida (1924-2002)

Known for his monumental sculptures, Chillida's approach to public art was shaped by the Mexican muralists' use of space and community engagement. He valued the integration of art into public spaces, similar to the Mexican tradition. Chillida's works often explore the relationship between form and space, drawing inspiration from the grand scale and social relevance of Mexican murals.

Walking along the streets of Puerto Vallarta, surrounded by such rich artistic heritage, feels like a rejuvenating spa for the mind and eyes. The city's vibrant art scene is a testament to the enduring influence of Mexican art and its power to inspire and captivate artists and art lovers from around the world.

OUR TIME / NUESTRO TIEMPO.
Lost-wax Bronze Casting
Dimension in meters: 2.06 (H) x 1.03 (W) x 0.66 (D)

ANTONIO RAMIREZ (1926-2010)
Mexican sculptor, painter and ceramic artist

His well-earned reputation as a teacher of several generations of artists justifies his pictorial production and place him in the important place of national and international art.

THE FOUNTAIN/ LA FUENTE
Lost-wax Bronze Casting
Dimension in meters: 1.21 (H) x 0.74 (W) x 0.62 (D)

ANTONIO RAMIREZ (1926-2010)
Mexican sculptor, painter and ceramic artist

LITTLE VENUS
Lost-wax Bronze Casting
Dimension in meters: 0.77 (H) x 0.3 (W) x 0.22 (D)

ANTONIO RAMIREZ (1926-2010)
Mexican sculptor, painter and ceramic artist

Kovay Gardens is a tranquil oasis, distinguished by its artistic flair, located in the stunning region of Bahia de Banderas, Nayarit, 30 minutes drive from Puerto Vallarta.

Works of art scattered throughout the resort, blending with natural beauty and chic architecture, offer a unique and enriching experience for art aficionados.

The container building at the Banderas Bay, Nayarit may be the most beautiful public washroom in the world.

Contemporary architecture in Mexico is renowned for its bold and innovative designs that seamlessly blend modern aesthetics with traditional elements and the natural environment.

The fine and unique natural environment nurtures a creative and artistic Mexico.

藝術之旅-巴亞爾塔港

在陽光明媚的日子抵達巴亞爾塔港，我同時感受到了撲面而來的熱空氣和濃郁的藝術氣息。

這座位於墨西哥太平洋沿岸的美麗沿海城市及其附近的小鎮充滿活力和創意。街頭巷尾到處是色彩繽紛的壁畫、異域風情的手工藝術品、時尚建築和富有藝術細胞的人們。

本文照片均為作者拍攝

墨西哥的壁畫、塗鴉和民間藝術是極富視覺衝擊的狂想曲。長期以來一直激發著世界各地藝術家的靈感：

巴勃羅·畢卡索 (1881-1973)

作為現代藝術的核心人物，畢卡索在西班牙內戰期間和之後的作品，尤其是《格爾尼卡》，與墨西哥藝術家的壁畫在主題和風格上有著共同的聯繫。與墨西哥藝術家作品的接觸，豐富了畢加索對超現實主義的探索。他欣賞墨西哥藝術家描繪社會鬥爭和人類苦難的方式，這些主題與他的作品有深刻的共鳴。

迭戈·裡維拉 (1886-1957)

裡維拉是當代著名的墨西哥畫家，他的壁畫推動了國際壁畫藝術思潮。裡維拉的作品深深植根於墨西哥文化和歷史，描繪了原住民的生活、殖民化的影響以及工人階級的鬥爭。他的壁畫出現在世界各地的公共場所，將墨西哥藝術帶給全球觀眾。

讓·夏洛 (1898-1979)

法國出生的藝術家讓·夏洛深受墨西哥壁畫主義和原住民藝術的影響。他與裡維拉的合作並融入墨西哥藝術界，這使他能夠將歐洲繪畫技巧與墨西哥藝術融合，創造出引起國際共鳴的獨特風格。

薩爾瓦多·達利 (1904-1989)

著名的西班牙超現實主義藝術家達利在他引人注目且夢幻般的作品中融入了墨西哥的影響。達利為 1939 年紐約世界博覽會設計了「維納斯之夢」展館，展示了融合各種文化影響的超現實環境，其中的元素讓人想起墨西哥藝術大膽和不拘一格的風格。達利對鮮豔色彩、奇幻意象和複雜象徵的運用與墨西哥藝術豐富的視覺語言相呼應。

弗里達·卡羅 (1907-1954)

弗里達·卡羅的眾多肖像、自畫像和受墨西哥自然環境及手工藝品啟發而創作的作品在世界各地廣為流傳並啟發了全球無數藝術家。她對鮮豔色彩的運用和融合墨西哥民間藝術傳統，使她成為墨西哥和女性主義藝術運動中的標誌性人物。

愛德華多·奇利達 (1924-2002)

奇利達以其紀念性雕塑而聞名，他對公共藝術的態度受到墨西哥壁畫家對空間的利用和社區參與的影響。他重視將藝術融入公共空間，這與墨西哥的傳統類似。奇利達從墨西哥壁畫的宏大規模和社會關連性中汲取靈感，因此他的作品經常探索形式與空間之間的關係。

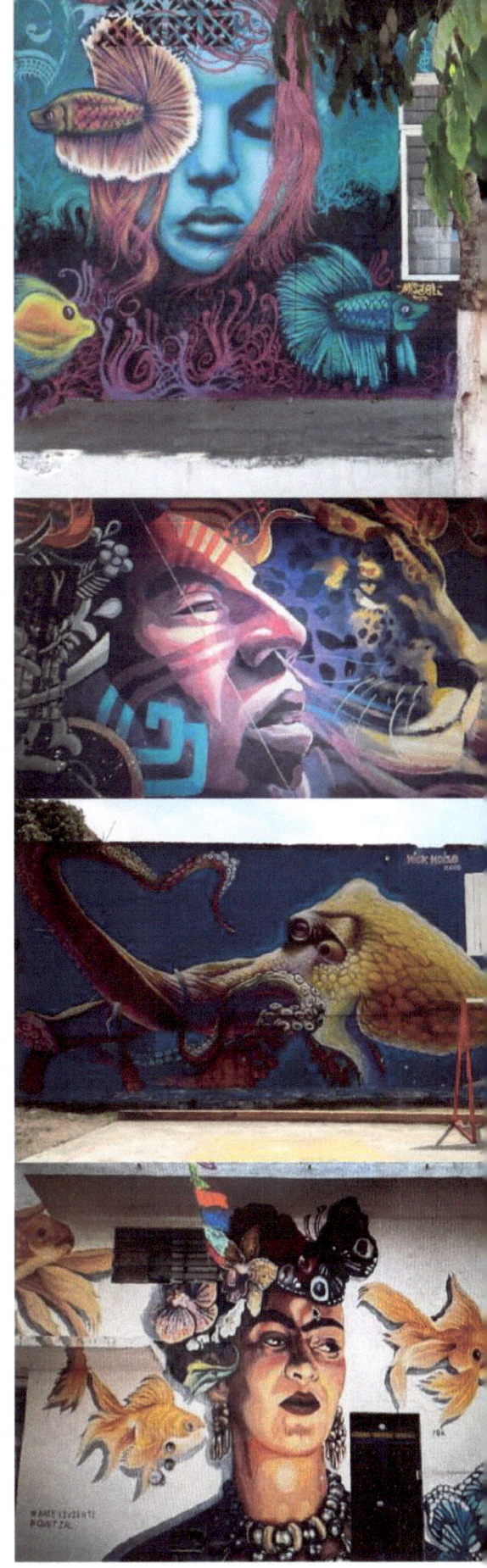

指繪畫家安东尼奧用食指創作瓷板畫

巴亞爾塔港之旅，沈浸於豐富多彩的藝術世界，是一趟心靈和視覺的洗禮。這應證了墨西哥藝術的影響力及吸引世界各地藝術家和藝術愛好者的魔力。

科瓦伊花园 (Kovay Gardens) 是一片宁静的绿洲,以其艺术气息而闻名,位于纳亚里特令人惊叹的巴伊亚·德·班德拉斯 (Bahia de Banderas) 地区,距离巴亚尔塔港 (Puerto Vallarta) 30 分钟车程。

艺术作品遍布整个度假村,与自然美景和别致的建筑融为一体,为艺术爱好者提供独特而丰富的体验。

我们的时间/NUESTRO TIEMPO
失蜡青铜铸件
规格(米):2.06(高)×1.03(宽)×0.66(深)

安东尼奥·拉米雷斯(1926-2010)
墨西哥雕塑家、画家和陶瓷艺术家

作为几代艺术家的导师,他赢得卓越声誉和国内外艺术界的重要地位

纳亚里特班德拉斯湾的集装箱建筑可能是世界上最美丽的公共卫生间。

墨西哥的当代建筑将现代美学与传统元素和自然环境无缝融合，並以其大胆创新的设计而闻名於世。

优美独特的自然环境孕育了富有创造力和艺术气息的墨西哥。

' When you discover the secret of appreciation, the world is different.'

-James B.S.

鑑賞家 CONNOISSEUR
DISCOVER ART OF APPRECIATION

www.ingramcontent.com/pod-product-compliance
Lightning Source LLC
Chambersburg PA
CBHW042055050526
44107CB00110B/1189